DAUGHTER MOTHER ME

In life, women can have many labels: daughter, wife, career woman, mother. Alana Kirk has worn them all; and, whilst her life is hectic, she feels in control. Then, four days after the birth of her third daughter, her mother suffers a massive stroke. And just like that, everything changes . . . Alana has entered what she terms her 'Sandwich Years' — sandwiched between seeing to the needs of her parents and children: both grieving for, and caring for, her beloved mum; supporting her father; raising her three young daughters; and getting her career back on track. But how long can she continue before the cracks begin to show?

First published in Great Britain in 2016 by
Hachette Books Ireland
Dublin

First Large Print Edition
published 2017
by arrangement with
Hachette UK Ltd
London

A catalogue record for this book is available
from the British Library.

ISBN 978–1–4448–3408–6

Published by
F. A. Thorpe (Publishing)
Anstey, Leicestershire

Set by Words & Graphics Ltd.
Anstey, Leicestershire
Printed and bound in Great Britain by
T. J. International Ltd., Padstow, Cornwall
This book is printed on acid-free paper

SPECIAL MESSAGE TO READERS

THE ULVERSCROFT FOUNDATION
(registered UK charity number 264873)

re   es.

Eye

eat

and
gy,

up,

ern

yal

on

Y   ou

]   r

Leicester LE7 7FU, England
Tel: (0116) 236 4325

website: www.foundation.ulverscroft.com

Alana Kirk is a writer and journalist. She has travelled the world, working for charities and telling their stories. Originally from Belfast, Alana now lives in Dublin. She works for the non-profit sector in addition to raising her three girls and writing.

Website — www.alanakirkwriting.com

Twitter — @AlanaKirkWords

To Mum . . . you will always be
holding my hand.

To Daisy, Poppy and Ruby Rose. . .
I will always be holding yours.

The 'Sandwich Years'
The term Sandwich Generation was aptly coined a decade or so ago to describe those of us who are literally sandwiched between the responsibility and care for children and parents. This multi-generational and multi-responsible caregiving is not new. Since caves were carved, a corner was always made for each generation. As the trend towards later parenting and longer life expectancy continues — and with more women playing an increasingly active role in the workforce — we are seeing a generation of women caught in a boiling pot of pressure that can have a hugely negative impact on their physical, emotional and mental health.
Alana Kirk

Contents

Introduction

We are all orphans-in-waiting.

From the moment we are born, we are destined to lose our parents. The questions are when and how.

The parent-care years don't come with an appointment card and a preparation pack. There is no go-to YouTube video. It is something that we often have to figure out as it happens. Perhaps it starts with a fall. Your mum or dad trips and breaks a hip, and you gradually realise they aren't as strong as they used to be. They are stumbling over a step, and you are stumbling into unknown territory. It could be a hospital appointment with a diagnosis that changes everything. Or even just a slowing down and reduced independence. It could be an awful, heart-breaking, slow mental deterioration that leaves you caring for a person who no longer knows who you are, while you deal with the loss and grief for the person they were.

Losing a parent — whether we are close to them or not, have had a great relationship with them or not, will miss them or not — is a catastrophic event in anyone's life.

For me, it happened at a very specific and challenging time, when, like many women, life was already packed with other responsibilities — marriage, career and children. The care years arrived by ambulance one night, four days after my third baby was born. I call them my Sandwich Years — sandwiched between caring for my parents and my young children.

However the parent-care years arrive — be they sandwiched or just open (with no children but still the responsibility of caring for parents) — they are filled with hardship, choices and horror. Hopefully they can also be filled with humour, love and growth.

Most of us are totally unprepared. Struggling under multi-generational, multi-care responsibilities, as well as carving our way through a life of relationships, career and interests, can threaten to suck away our very identity. This book tells my specific journey of how I lost myself in the mayhem and slowly fought to find a way back to me.

Coming to terms with the role-reversal of caring for your parent, dealing with the needs of your own family figuring out the practical issues of care while coping with the emotional fallout of grief and fear can make these Sandwich Years a very challenging time.

Modern life has removed many of the

burdens women before us endured. The sheer act of washing clothes used to be a two-day event. Every week. Now we can work, play and live our lives with greater freedom to have our children later in life. Older people are now not older until they are *much* older. Modern life and feminist ferocity have enabled women today to have choices, make choices, live choices that have transformed our lives.

But sometimes we are left with no choice.

Many women are finding themselves overworked, overextended, overstressed and over a barrel. The demands on our time, the emotional wringing out, the guilt at feeling you are constantly short-changing someone, can be overwhelming. When the two book-ends of our lives need us at the same time, we have little choice but to slot in between. Our parents may need us for all kinds of reasons — mental deterioration, physical illness or just old age — but the pain of grieving while dealing with the grim reality of their diminishing life is a challenge few of us are ever prepared for.

I certainly wasn't. This book is not a how-to manual, it's just my story. And while the Sandwich Generation is a growing demographic, every situation is different.

Every parental relationship is challenging

in different ways. We have all had parents once and whether we now love them or hate them, disown them or still live with them, can call them friends or are just embarrassed by them, when they start to depend on us, it has a significant impact on our lives. You might be a full-time carer, a part-time carer or share the caring with your siblings. Your experience may involve very practical and personally intimate levels of care, or may be simply (but not easily) emotional support. It will almost certainly involve shock, fear and grief. You are often, and at the same time, also dealing with the demands of your own family and trying to stretch your care over a range of needs. Guilt will put his arm around you and become your constant companion. Between the juggling, the guilt and the relentless choices to be made, it is easy to lose track of your own identity.

This book is about accepting the reality and adapting to a new way of life, about reaching out for help and finding the supports you need to keep going; and about finding the standards that will keep everything steady while also keeping you sane. But, ultimately, it's about rediscovering yourself amid this maelstrom of need, and welcoming joy and learning back into your life.

Daughter, Mother, Me began life as a blog

I called 'The Sandwich Years' in 2011, as a place to express my joy and grief, my loss and love, my frustrations and anger and hope, my struggles and muddles as I negotiated these uncharted waters. The term 'Sandwich Generation' describes those caught up in the dual responsibilities of caring for children and parents. As I wrote, often in the dark of night when the needs of those who depended on me had receded only a little, I got responses from people from all over the world who were perhaps experiencing some or all of the pressures I was feeling, or maybe even more. Many people had much harder situations to deal with than I did, and I took support from them.

I was not alone. And that is an important thing to know. Because life can be a testing old witch, and sometimes she just throws stuff at you for the fun of it. Knowing there are others fire-fighting the same issues really helps.

As time drew on, and I began to fill in the details and explore the Sandwich Years, this book became a celebration of a special mother-daughter relationship with my mum, which shines a guiding light on the daughter-mother relationships with my girls. I hope it is also a celebration of women and friendships and love.

This book is for the everyday warriors. Not the famous women in magazines, not the tanned and the airbrushed, but the saggy-arsed, the rotund of tum, the fit and the lean, the round and robust; for the women who care constantly for other people, and in doing so keep humanity human. This is for women who, despite juggling it all, still find time to pour a glass of wine for a friend in tears. This is for the women who get up day after day after day and put their faces on and light up lives, even when theirs feel dark. As I have discovered, the only way we can make it through this old thing called life is with love, and help and great women and great men around us.

I have spent the Sandwich Years so far squeezed to my limits. It's been hard. But then I look at the woman and girls I'm sandwiched between and feel very lucky indeed.

Alana Kirk, December 2015

1

Caught in the Perfect Storm of Care

Happiness and horror. There should probably be a decompression tank between them — a space to come down from the high before you plummet to the depths. But life isn't like that. It comes in a box with no instructions and no special space to hide. You just have to take deep breaths whenever you can. This can be hard for someone like me. I'm a planner. Some people call it a condition. I call it good sense. I like to plan (colour-coordinated on a spreadsheet if possible). I like Post-It notes. I like coloured pens. I LOVE highlighter markers. But I have learned to accept that every day when I pull back the curtains and search for a glimpse of the sky, I have no idea what will happen. There are no aeroplane banners flapping in the wind telling me what will happen outside of my colour-coded list system. But on a bright day in September 2010, I didn't need aerial acrobatics to leave a message in the jet stream that day. I already knew what was going to happen. I was going to have a baby.

Such an ordinary, everyday event. Some 2 billion million are born every minute (possibly not an accurate figure), yet for every one of those 2 billion million mothers, it is an extraordinary, primeval, earth-shattering, life-changing event. On this sunny September day, I would meet my new daughter, airlifted out in an orderly fashion through a scheduled C-section.

There was great excitement in our house. My other two daughters couldn't wait to meet their new sister. Daisy was four and had started school three weeks earlier. She was finding the change a little daunting and I was still peeling her fingers off the front door in the mornings. Poppy was three and had just started Montessori. She was used to bringing her 'baby' doll (which she had named a rather charming Glitzy Rosie) into the classroom with her. She had the impression my new baby would be no different.

'Can I bring the new baby in with me tomorrow?' she asked. 'Teacher will put her on the shelf while we work.'

'We might wait a few weeks,' I told her, already dubious about the immediate safety of this new baby.

My mum and dad had arrived down from Belfast the night before in a flurry of Christmas-Eve-like excitement. Instead of hanging my stocking, I packed my hospital bag, anticipation twinkling like glitter in my stomach. Later, I would be unwrapping one of the best gifts of my life.

That morning, the September sun was sitting bold and gold in a pale blue cushion sky. My husband brought me my morning cup of tea, and the girls scurried into my room and huddled and cuddled under my duvet. Mum popped her head around the bedroom door and our eyes smiled at each other. I could hear Dad pottering downstairs and the cat was probably purring at my feet and the dog sniffing my slippers under the bed. I'm pretty sure, if I think back hard enough, there was dreamy music filtering through the air, and George Clooney was washing my car bare-chested in the driveway.

Having a pre-planned C-section adds a certain calmness to the whole childbirth challenge. My initial dreams of an organic, breath-through-the-pain, grin-and-grit, natural birth went up in a puff of epidural when Daisy was born. My colour-coded birthplan had drifted to the floor (to be stamped on by running staff who left bloody footprints on the section that said 'Natural Delivery') as they whipped me to theatre for an emergency C-section, and I'm not sure I ever got a grip on parenting again. Poppy was born two years later but any plans I might have had of being in control of *that* situation were laughingly dashed when she turned out to be a frank breech (her bum down with her feet around her ears, no chance of ever getting her bottom anywhere out of my bottom), so another C-section was required. That was, unless I wanted to be buying nappies for the both of us over the next few years.

And now, finally, baby number three. Apparently it isn't natural to have a baby squeezed out when two have been airlifted, so a natural birth was ruled out. Something about rupturing. I let go of my dream and made a grab for continence.

So at 8.30 that morning, Mum and I left behind the filtered music, cuddling girls, pottering Dad, tea-making husband, purring cat, sniffing dog and bare-chested George Clooney and headed to the hospital. My husband took the girls to school and went into work for a couple of hours. Mum would stay with me for all the pre-surgery hanging around bit and then he would come in for the main show. Mum and I were good at hanging around together. We could chit over the chat long after our pot of Earl Grey tea had gone cold.

Mum sat with me in the pre-op waiting room for several hours. I kept rubbing my tummy. Mum kept rubbing my tummy. In a few short hours, a little person would emerge. A whole real, fought-for person. The wonder of new life never gets old. To while away the time, Mum painted my nails. Childbirth peels dignity away from you like a banana skin. I knew I'd soon be peeing into a bag and wearing paper pants to hold in the enormous pads they make you wear. The very least I could do was wear lipstick and nail varnish.

Apparently not. Nail varnish is a dignity too far.

As soon as Mum had finished and I held up my hands in admiration, the nurse swooped into view. She was holding out a bottle of nail varnish remover and cotton wool pads. And a rather smug smile.

Off came the nail varnish.

The clock ticked slowly. My heart beat fast. Mum held my hand steady. She had always held my hand. Even when I reached adulthood, she would feel the need to take my hand crossing the road. I think she just believed I would always be her baby, needing her protection. But I suspect that somewhere along the way, she took my hand less for her to get me across the road, and more for me to get her across. Either way, we had got to the stage where we helped each other.

This was somehow fine again in my forties,

but it had been mortifying when she'd visited me at university. Yes, she'd taken my hand as we crossed the main campus square in front of everyone I knew. Wearing Doc Martens and holding your mum's hand as you walked into the Nelson Mandela café is not a look that inspires street cred. If I had to choose one memory to sum up my relationship with my mum, it would be the two of us holding hands.

So we held hands and rubbed my tummy and smiled. I asked the nurse to take a photo of us. I have it beside my bed now. Mum looks like she always did. Kind and warm. Her hair coiffed to sit perfectly around her face. Her bright cornflower-blue eyes smiling wider than her lipsticked mouth. A neat blue jumper lifted by simple gold jewellery. She is beautiful.

Just after 2 p.m. the nurse came over.

'It's time for you to go into the theatre now.'

I hugged my mum and told her I would see her on the other side. She hugged me back and told me she loved me, something she had done every day of my life. She said she would come back later that night to meet her new granddaughter (and repaint my nails). My husband had arrived and, together, we headed towards the operating rooms, smiles bigger than our faces. Maybe I looked out the window as I walked towards the theatre. If only there had been a plane-trailing banner in the sky. If only I could have read the jet stream. In just four days, something would happen and my mum would never be able to say she loved me again.

★　★　★

I'm not sure why I had wanted my mum there that day. Serendipity, perhaps. When the events of the week did unfold I was so grateful that we had shared that last wonderful experience together.

Just as she had done with my other two daughters, Mum had planned to stay with me and help in those exhausting first few weeks after Ruby came home from hospital.

When Daisy was born, Mum and Dad had leapt into their car the moment I'd told them I was in labour. They were still on the M1 driving down from Belfast when we texted to say their granddaughter had been born by emergency C-section. For me, that evening was a fug of drugs but I remember my mum's face, her hand stroking mine, and her look of love when she held my first child. That next morning, Mum had arrived into my hospital room with a hug and a pot of homemade blackberry jam. I was all pain and pleasure. Amid the euphoria I had felt at finally meeting my first daughter, I was also aching and fragile. I had been sliced open, after all. Contemplating getting out of bed to wash, never mind pulling off and on clothes over my stitched and sore body, had been too awful to consider. But Mum had been making me wash since I'd been, well, a child, so she'd coaxed me to take a shower.

She had helped me take the tentative steps to the bathroom, and helped me take off my nightdress. She'd gently pulled the plastic band of my paper pants over my wound and pulled them off, my hand holding her head. She'd supported my weight as I stepped over the bath and under the shower. She'd gently hosed me over with the soothing warm water and reverently sponged the soap around my bruised body. Then, after helping me out, she'd rubbed the towel over my legs and back, and softly patted dry my wound and dressing.

At seventy-one, my mother was still caring for her baby. At thirty-six, I had been just about to start learning how to take care of mine. I knew then my journey as a parent would never end. It was for life, just as my mum's mothering of me was for hers. Two things had happened simultaneously the day

14

Daisy was born. I became a mother, and I became a daughter all over again. And the unbreakable bond I'd formed with my beautiful new baby shone a light on the bond I already held with my beautiful old mum.

Over the years that followed, as I loved and struggled with parenting, first Daisy and then Poppy, realising now the relentless tough slog that motherhood is, I had renewed respect for how hard my mum must have worked to bring up my brother and me, and how thankless a job it must have been at times. My dad's generation wasn't in the business of babies, and she didn't have all those modern amenities that make my workload barely tolerable — baby monitors, tumble dryers, disposable nappies and microwaves. I was just about keeping my head above water as it was — how would I have coped without a dishwasher? Daytime cartoons? A downstairs loo?

Before Daisy was born, I had only remembered my mum as a mother to a stroppy child, a wilful teenager, a wild twenty-something, and an independent thirty-something. But when I became a parent, and watched as she tenderly cared for my girls, I appreciated how she must have been as a mother to me when I was a baby. As she radiated love for them, humming lullabies, stroking their tiny faces, making

15

them giggle and reading them endless stories, I realised how loved I must have been. She walked beside me as I pushed the pram around the streets to get Daisy to sleep, singing the same songs she had sung to me, teaching me the words of motherhood so that I could sing them to my own children. My mum had an annoying habit when I was growing up of saying, 'You wait, you'll understand when you have kids of your own!' As I stropped out of the house in an adolescent huff or threw a teenage tantrum, I'd raise my eyes to the sky and bemoan the endless words of caution, the beratings and instructions on how to behave. These days I raise my eyes to the sky and when I open my mouth, my mother comes out. In becoming a mother, I have become *my* mother. That used to make her laugh a lot. Payback is smiling into your tea while your daughter is being shredded by your stubborn granddaughter.

When I was growing up, we fought. We fought a lot. Slammed doors and snorts of snideness were the percussion to our relationship. But the melody was the hot pour of Earl Grey tea, soft banter and the whisper of touching skin. The 'baa baa' of a new baby did not change the fact that Mum could still make me gaga. We still argued, and I still threw my eyes up to the skies. But at the end of a long day when I'd put my girls to bed, I would come down the stairs to hear my mum fussing in a newly cleaned kitchen, knowing that for a few hours that evening I'd be fed and hugged and probably berated. Which was OK because while learning to be a mother, I still very much needed to be *mothered*. And so it was again, for the first few days in hospital, as I got to know my newest daughter, I got to be Mum's daughter again as she looked after my other girls and came in to see me every evening to look after me, too.

★　★　★

Just four days after Ruby was born, I pulled back the curtains in search of a glimpse of the sky. It was there, in all its hazy beauty. But life was lurking behind clouds of gloom. And it was holding a grenade. I had been cocooned with my baby in a small hospital room; a womb for us both before we emerged into the bright lights of the real world. Each day my husband had arrived, his smile chasing the ears off his face. Each day he had brought in our two girls, who thought Ruby was a doll. They'd played with her for a moment, taken all her clothes off and then left her dangling off the bed. And each day my mum and dad had brought me a treat. On the first day, I got my usual pot of blackberry jam to eat with my breakfast and, over the next few days, it was ice-cream or chocolate.

But on my last day I told everyone to stay away. I was coming home the next day and, to be honest, I needed to rest. I wanted time with my precious new little girl before the madness of mothering three under-fives got underway. So my husband took my parents and girls out for the day, and I nestled in my hospital cocoon, sleeping and feeding and smiling.

Until the doctor came in and catastrophe struck.

I was in that muddled mist of half-sleep, lying on my bed, Ruby wrapped in my arms. I started awake and tried to pull myself to sitting (not easy when you have eighteen stitches across your belly and a sleeping baby in your arms). I smiled, the doctor smiled; everyone smiles around a baby. We talked and he stepped closer. He looked at Ruby and stopped smiling. So I stopped smiling and looked at Ruby.

I gasped. A huge coagulated blob of blood blazed across her perfect soft fuzzy head. I heard his sharp intake of breath, his arms reaching out for her. For some reason, my instinct was to pull her closer to me and it was then I had a funny feeling. I looked closer and my smile returned. Concern turned to confusion on his face, confusion turned to comprehension on my face.

I skimmed my finger along Ruby's head, scooping up the dark red residue.

'Ah,' I said, taking a lick. 'That'll be a dollop of my mum's blackberry jam.'

Catastrophe averted.

How Mum laughed when I told her on the phone that evening. We spoke about me coming home the next morning and she told me what a wonderful day she'd had with Daisy and Poppy. As we ended the call, she was off to read my girls a story and put them to bed. They were very giddy at the thought of me bringing their little sister home. She told me she loved me. All was good in the world. But the clouds were gathering, and none of us thought to look out the window.

I settled down for the evening, knowing that the following day, I'd carry a baby from this hospital for the last time, and that the rest of my life would begin as I danced off across a meadow of wild flowers. This was clearly the last fumes of the drugs taking effect. Or the hormones. Despite having already had two babies, I had forgotten that what would really happen was that I would carry a baby home from hospital and life would be swamped by a tsunami of sleepless insanity and lurid green poo.

Once I knew Mum would have put the girls to bed, I waited for the texts. What's the answer to three down? Have I worked out seventeen across? That's how Mum and I did the *Irish Times* crossword — usually with her in Belfast, me in Dublin — a texting triumph of collaboration. But no texts came.

My husband came instead.

I was asleep, trying to get a couple of hour's rest before the next feed at 2 a.m. Suddenly the door to my room crashed open and the lights crashed on. I saw him standing in the doorway and, for a horrible second, I thought it was morning already and I'd slept through the night without feeding Ruby. I glanced at her but saw her sleeping soundly, fully hydrated and content. But then my eyes flicked back to the door fearfully. I knew then, the moment I saw his expression, that my life had just changed forever. No words will ever express the sorrow and horror on his face. In the three seconds it took for him to walk from the door to my bedside, frantic glimpses of family flashed in my brain — Daisy, Poppy, Mum, Dad, my brother — so that when he got to my side and took my hand, all I could say was, 'Who is it?'

He bowed his head for a second before he broke my world. 'It's your mum.'

★   ★   ★

A nurse found me a wheelchair and my husband found me a doctor who would discharge me at midnight. My husband had taken my mum to hospital as soon as he realised she was having a stroke and she had been sick in the car. He had called my friend Amanda to mind the children before coming to tell me. I left one hospital and while I was being driven to another in a car that stank of my mum's vomit, I called my brother Simon.

'It's Mum . . . ' was all I could manage, before handing the phone to my husband so that he could explain. The pain in my stomach screamed with the effort the journey was taking but the pain in my heart screamed louder. We had buckled Ruby's car seat in the back, hurriedly, without thought, without balloons, without fanfare. This was not how it was supposed to be. Happiness had flipped to horror and she was already experiencing the whiplash.

I could barely walk the distance from the car to A&E. I thought I was going to vomit with the pain. Someone found me a wheelchair and my husband pushed me to the main area. My eyes searched desperately for my mum. But amidst all the mayhem and noise, the only likely person I could see was an old woman, at least 154 years old, lying wild-eyed, open-mouthed, her face as grey as her hair. I looked around, clutching my baby because the place screamed 'Germs!' My husband brought me towards the old woman.

Why are you bringing me here? I thought, and then I saw the old man beside her. It was my dad.

Why is he sitting here with this old woman? I thought, and then I saw what he was holding. It was my mum's hand.

Why is Mum's hand on that woman? I thought and then I realised who the old woman was.

How could this happen? We'd had a plan. The plan was for me to come out of hospital and live happily ever after. And yet here I was. Wiping pieces of vomit from around her mouth, while trying to find the woman I knew in her eyes.

My dad had collapsed into himself. He looked like one of those carcasses on the African plains reduced to skin and skeleton. My head was still trying to come to terms with what was happening. A stroke, we were told. How could this be? I had only spoken to her! She does water aerobics twice a week! Two hours before she had been reading my girls a story, her rose-coloured lipstick intact. How can this old, grey creature be my mum?

Where is my mum? Where is my mum! Talk to me, Mum. But for the first time in my life, her eyes were silent.

Ruby started to cry and I realised she needed feeding. But how could I feed her? Every ounce of my energy, every cell in my body was focused on my mum, willing her to wake up, stop this nonsense, put some lipstick on and hold my hand. We'd have a nice cup of Earl Grey tea and a 'little bit of something nice'. This is what my mum had always said when we shared a cup of tea. 'Sure we have to have a little bit of something nice to go with it.' This usually involved chocolate. Instead, I gripped her hand and eventually a nurse suggested I go and feed Ruby in a little room. It wasn't safe for her here. She hadn't had any vaccinations yet and the A&E was a breeding ground for everything that a newborn baby doesn't want to get.

And there it was. That first awful decision. My baby or my mother. Reluctantly I left my mum to feed my baby. I took Ruby into a side room and fed her, but then I immediately went back to Mum, leaving my husband to wind Ruby. Five days of never leaving my baby's side were broken as I went to the person who had never left mine. Guilt had crept silently into the hospital, put his arm around my shoulders, and was now lingering by my side. I needed to support my old mum, and I needed to support my new daughter, and suddenly the brutality of that choice pulled at my very skin. I wasn't to know these constant choices would rip the skin from my flesh over the coming years. But, for now, in those first few hours, it was just horror. And it got worse.

We heard him before we saw him. Flailing and punching, as they wheeled his bed into the slot next to Mum in the A&E ward. He smelled of anger and that horrible combination of ripe drink and stale cigarettes. He was a one-man show of abuse and profanity. He lashed out with his fists at the doctors trying to help him and lashed out with his tongue at the nurses trying to quieten him. He had been stabbed in the head and wanted everyone to know about it.

I cradled my mum's head, whispering in her ear, trying to drown out his voice. Her own mouth opened and closed but no sound came out. The man was screeching four-, five- and even some choice six-letter curses, and I was getting more and more panicked that that would be the last thing my mum ever heard. I thought she was going to die, but this awful man kept screaming and I kept whispering until, at one point, I simply put my hands over Mum's ears, sobbing into her barely moving chest, the smell of her Estée Lauder *Beautiful* still warm on her skin. It was the smell of the love that had always blanketed me. And it woke me up.

I started in a low mumble. 'Please be quiet. Please be quiet. Please be quiet.' My voice got stronger. I turned to his curtain. 'Please, my mum is dying. Please be quiet.'

I looked around me. A sterile, busy, frantic, awful A&E ward. How can you end your life here? My mum loved the sea, loved views, loved walking along a beach collecting shells. She loved music. That's how she needed to die. Not in this room. Not with this man shouting and swearing. Not on this day. Please, not on this day.

'Please. Please, can you be quiet, my mum is here and you need to be quiet.'

He kept going, he kept going, he kept going, and I could feel the tension in me rise. He kept going, his angry, whiney voice rising and rising, along with the fist in my stomach. He just kept shouting and swearing that he'd been stabbed in the head.

I broke. I broke away and I tore towards him before anyone could stop me.

'SHUT UP OR I'LL STAB YOU IN THE HEAD MYSELF!' I screamed (also inserting a few choice swear words to match his).

Silence descended like a white ward sheet.

25

I knew people were looking at me. But I was a woman with a wound and a newborn baby, so they said nothing and turned away. It only stunned him quiet for a moment, before he started up again, but thankfully two gardai arrived and he was wheeled away.

I slunk back beside my mum (as well as you can slink when your stomach is stitched together and your mind is falling apart). My husband brought Ruby out to me because she needed another feed and I picked up my precious little bundle of new life and held her up beside my precious larger bundle of fading life, three generations of skin touching, three generations of genes blending, three generations of love entwining. With me sandwiched in the middle.

Soon, they told us her bed on the stroke ward was ready. I can still picture the caravan of catastrophe that went tumbling along next, like a freak-show troupe. In front of me, my mum was being wheeled in a bed down a corridor with my shrunken dad walking beside her; behind her, I was being wheeled in a chair, my four-day-old baby on my lap, crying to be fed.

I looked at my mum, and I looked at my baby.

I had just been enveloped into a perfect storm of need.

There was no George Clooney. Just decisions and choices and care that would nearly break my bones. I had entered what I would call my Sandwich Years.

2

The Aftermath

'The first twenty-four hours are critical.' This is what we were told. But, critical for whom? The term didn't just apply to my mum. They were critical for everyone who loved and depended on her. That night, as soon as she was settled in the ward, I sat with her until the new dawn broke, Ruby still in the car seat at my feet. I didn't dare look at the other patients lying in the surrounding beds, in case they got up and started walking towards us, arms outstretched like zombies. That's what they looked like, half-dead creatures from a bad horror movie.

I drew the curtain around Mum in case she woke up and saw them too, and thought she had already died.

In the quiet of the ward I was able to look at her calmly for the first time. If my dad was a carcass on an African plain, then my mum was a long, half-formed shadow cast from a high, burning sun. She had been a life force and now she was barely alive. I probably looked like a half-eaten deer caught in the headlights of a lion's stare. Only there was no fight or flight, just fright.

My brother arrived red-eyed after his red-eye flight from Edinburgh, grey with shock. I placed Mum's hand from mine into his and went home to see my girls. I was momentarily stunned to see the 'Welcome Home' bunting hanging pink and poignant across the front door. I had forgotten that just hours earlier our lives had been all about happiness. I was meant to be bringing home my new baby with Mum and Dad welcoming me in the doorway. Now life was filled with horror. The joy of what was meant to be compounded the grief of what now was, as the bunting swayed in the breeze.

The girls, still unaware, screamed with excitement when my husband and I walked in with Ruby, and I had to remember to smile when I saw them. They fussed and fumbled over their new sister, their squeals like a sprinkling of sparkle in a deep, dense mist. But I just stood dazed, crazed with shock and exhaustion. My mum's cardigan was hanging over the banister. Her shoes were by the door. I didn't know it yet, but she would never wear either again.

I sobbed as I put Mum's hospital bag together. Being in 'Nanna's room', which our spare room was affectionately called because my mum stayed there so much, was like standing in a hail of sharp knives. The book she had been reading was on the bedside table, a bookmark made by Daisy sticking out and showing it was only half-read. The *Irish Times* crossword was on the bed, unfinished and, beside it, her small navy leather handbag. Her clothes hung in the wardrobe, her smell hung in the air. I had no idea what to pack for someone whose life had been so brutally interrupted. I threw in her deep rose nail varnish. There must always be nail varnish. I went to get her handbag, but then stopped. I couldn't face looking inside. There would be notes and endless lists covered in her neat handwriting. Her lipstick. Her wallet and her photos. I knew every item in her handbag as intimately as I knew my own. I left it unopened. She wouldn't be needing it any time soon.

Life decided to give me a little break on that day it broke me. If I had opened that handbag, and lifted out her notebook, and read one particular piece of paper, I think I would have collapsed into the arms of grief until they squeezed me to death. It would be days before I could summon the strength to open her bag. I thought the pain would be in just seeing her things. Things she would never use again. But something made me wait.

Something made me not see what she had written yet because, although my mum couldn't talk anymore, she would speak to me again, just when I needed it.

* * *

After lunch, when I had showered and spent a little time with the girls, I returned to the hospital. The walk from the entrance to Mum's ward was still too difficult for me, so I had to be pushed in a wheelchair.

At one point, I wondered if there was a spare bed for me.

The nurses must have washed Mum's face and mouth, and put a new nightie on her, but it seemed they had also washed her of colour. She lay grey and motionless, locked in a silent hell. The previous night, the doctors had told us that, at that moment, she was paralysed. Mute. Probably brain damaged. Suddenly, her eyes opened and saw mine. They screamed for me to help her. I held her hand but I think it was more to anchor myself because my instinct was to run from those eyes. Eyes that had always held me, now barely seemed to recognise me. Thankfully, they closed again.

About an hour later, when they opened again, I was almost afraid to look but, this time, they loved me so intensely I felt the earth shudder. My world had been transformed by two of the people I loved most in the world, my mum and my baby. Both were open to me only through their eyes. Neither could speak or move without my help. I was already feeling the weight of knowing that I had to find strength from somewhere to look in their eyes, to bring my baby out and bring my mum back.

But I didn't know how to bring her back. I was terrified she had gone somewhere I'd never find her. I thought she was going to die, that day or the next, and as I sat shellshocked beside her, all I could think of was the book beside her bed. Mum loved Rosamunde Pilcher's *The Shell Seekers* and she was reading it again. But she wasn't finished yet. And neither was I. My brain worked frantically, while every other part of me had stopped. *How can I live in a world where she is not? I've never done it before. I don't want to do it now. I don't ever want to do it. Not now. Not today. Not this year. Not this lifetime.* I gripped her hand, and my eyes screamed back at hers, *You're not done, Mum! Not by a long shot.*

She may have been in her seventies but isn't that the new fifties? She was fit and did water aerobics twice a week. Walked every day. She knitted my children cardigans and had a more active social life than I did. She never left the house without lipstick. She never mixed black and brown clothes. Everything matched and was neat. My brain just kept talking.

I'm a young mum. I am too young to lose my mum.

Who will call me every morning to see how my night was?

Who will I call every afternoon to hear how her day was?

Who will tell me how cold it is, even when it's 20 degrees and stone-splitting sun?

Who will call me every evening during the kids' tea, saying, 'I know it's a bad time . . . but . . . ' and then carry on talking?

Who will fix my knitting?

Who will turn their face to the sun with me as we sit outside and listen to the girls play?

Who will hold my hand to get me across the road?

Who will stroke my face?

Who will tell me I'm talented and amazing?

Who will tell me I'm spoiled and need to grow up?

Who will I call when I can't make gravy?

Who will look after me when I'm sick?

Who will I share everyday moments with over a cup of Earl Grey and a chocolate and have them say (every time), 'Ah shall we just have a little bit of something nice?'

I sat bolt upright. I still don't know how to stack the dishwasher properly! When I left home, I had just assumed you put the dishes in and closed the door. But apparently not. There is 'The Technique'. The Technique is not written anywhere, but it is a Technique that apparently I wasn't told about. Except, as I grasped her hand, I realised I had been told about it. A million times. By her. But I was always too busy to listen. Too annoyed to observe The Technique. I always thought I knew a Better Technique. One that involved No Technique. *So, Mum, you can't go! My eyes pleaded with her. I haven't learned The Technique yet. My dishwasher will forever be stacked incorrectly!*

The gravy! I still don't know how to make that. And knitting! I can cast on but you always cast off! And the cooker top. I never clean the cooker top and you always do, every time you come down to Dublin to see me, and now you won't ever come down again. I'm not ready! You need to show me! I have three children under five! I need you! They need you! They need you to lie in bed when you visit. I will hear their little footsteps patter past my door and into 'Nanna's room', and later I will go in, and they will be snuggled with you under the duvet like I used to do, and you will be reading to them or stroking their faces. Ruby needs you to sing her your songs. You haven't taught me all your songs yet. I don't know any songs! Only 'A — You're Adorable' and even with that I still get the tune wrong! I need more songs!

I needed more time. They were saying the next twenty-four hours would be critical. But they didn't understand. The next twenty-four years were critical. I needed my mum to help me be a mother.

The shock was like nothing I had ever experienced before. That night, when I staggered in from the hospital, I put the girls to bed and cuddled them tight, unable to hide the fear and the tears in my eyes. I had told them earlier in the day that Nanna was ill and that was why I had to go back to hospital. Now I was home, they had questions.

'Is Nanna very sick?' Daisy asked, her face solemn, unsure, seeing me so fragile.

'Yes,' I replied simply.

'Is she going to die?' she whispered.

I shuddered.

Twenty-four hours earlier my mum had spoken to me on the phone, laughing, happy and a vibrant part of my life. In twenty-four hours she could be gone forever.

'Maybe. Possibly,' I whispered back.

'Are you going to die?' she then asked, her world reduced to the worst thing she could imagine.

'No,' I smiled. Yes, I thought.

Later, I stood in the dark of my bedroom, unable to fathom what was happening. I had never lived in a world my mum had not, but now my world was reduced to the worst thing I had always imagined. The shock of it was physical. I started to shake and before I had time to think, I was retching into the toilet. Later my husband held me as I sobbed but the tears didn't wash away my fears. Those fears crept all over me so my very skin seemed to crawl with the agony of my shock and the beginnings of grief.

★   ★   ★

Mum survived the next twenty-four hours, but then she deteriorated.

That first day, my dad, brother and I had sat with her all afternoon and into the evening. It was clear she had suffered a catastrophic stroke. In fact, it was caused by a brain haemorrhage which led to massive bleeding in her brain. Brain damage was certain, she was unable to speak and her body had suffered too. She was completely paralysed down her right side, and was unable to swallow. In the strike of a clock's second hand, the stroke had struck her down completely. But that evening, she was stable enough that we were eventually told to go home.

Despite the men in my family being quiet while the women chatter on, we had always been a family that sat around and talked. My dad is a one-man show of one-liners and witty wordplays, while my brother keeps a low Northern Irish lilt for wit and wisdom rather than getting into idle chatter.

My childhood holiday memories involve endless nights (and sometimes days, when the weather was awful) sitting around a table or a fire playing Monopoly or cards in amiable chat. Or heated discussion. Our family did plenty of shouting. Either in a cottage in Donegal or camping in a tent on the Antrim coast, we sat around, my mum's Tupperware box of home-baked goodies being passed between us.

When Simon and I left and grew homes of our own, we still all got together for a week, or sometimes two, every year as an extended family. For my mum's seventieth a few years before all of this, we all went to Tuscany for a fortnight, a place she had always dreamed of visiting. And like old times, we sat around in the evening playing cards and passing around words with the wine.

But on this night, with Mum missing so starkly from the family, Dad, Simon and I just sat silently around my kitchen table. There was very little any of us could bear to say. Grief is an incredibly personal experience and even though we were going through our shared shock over what had happened, it was something we each had to endure as individuals. We started to make phone calls to family and friends, and, in our broken hearts, we knew with each call that we were breaking more.

The next few days were a blur of exhaustion, grief, fear and a chronic, crippling crush of powerlessness as we sat at Mum's bedside. My husband heroically managed everything with the house and girls, and not a day went by when there wasn't a pot of something to eat left on our doorstep by my friends. People can help. People can put their arm around you. People can make you tea. But nothing and nobody can take away the pain.

On the third day, I walked into the ward and found Mum's bed empty. I stood, fright-frozen. But a nurse quickly guided me to a single room where Mum lay, still tied to drips, which she kept ripping out with the hand she could use, and oxygen through her nose, which she also kept ripping out. When I saw the bright private room I was delighted. How nice! It was only with a jolt that I realised it was to give us privacy while she died.

That day the doctor sat Dad and me down in a small consultation room and asked us what we wanted to do if she stopped breathing. We didn't even look at each other. 'Do not intervene,' we both said. We knew Mum would hate to be left like this. It was one of her greatest fears. As she had cared for her own parents, and then seen the impact of age on some of her own friends, she'd been horrified and frightened by the indignity of it all. The incontinence. The pads. 'Never let me end up like that!' she had cried, many's the time. The doctors were preparing us for the worst but she began to stabilise and then improve.

After a couple of days, she was moved back onto the main ward in the stroke unit. She had begun to open her eyes a little, utter small unintelligible words with a low, small voice. But I couldn't read what her eyes were saying and I couldn't make out what her voice was saying. The Mum I knew had gone, and in her place was a grey, silent woman who couldn't move or eat and who barely spoke. But when everything is taken away, the smallest things matter. I was allowed to give her her first sip of Earl Grey tea. In actual fact it was 'thickened tea' which is made from tea and granules to make it viscous enough for stroke patients to sip without choking them. I tried to ignore that I was making her sip tea soup, but she took it to her mouth and swallowed. She didn't say what she had always said. Her eyes told me nothing would be a treat again. But it was still a little bit of something nice, and in a world of horror, it was a moment of happiness.

I found it hard to see her so old and worn. My mum had always made such an effort with her appearance and so I frantically tried to brush her hair and make her look nice, but there was no response from her. After a week or so, the nurses put her in a special chair that would support her weight and enable her to sit upright, so we could sit side by side. But she was so vacant, it almost felt worse. I'm a solutions person. A list person. But there was no solution here. Nothing a to-do list would fix. I got my love of lists from Mum. It would be rare for us to sit down without some sort of list being made. Mum would be horrified with the life she had now been left with. She was still with me, but she was gone from me too. I kept picking up the phone to call her. I would call her mobile to hear her voice on her voicemail message. Because I couldn't bear to hear the mumbles of her new voice. She seemed so lost and confused. We were told she would never walk again. Her right arm was contorted and dead, the hand that had stroked me and held me and baked with me would forever now be curled in a claw.

The hand that had written thousands of notes — like the one I found in her handbag a couple of days later.

I had just fed Ruby and put her down to sleep. I don't know why I didn't just lie down on the floor of her bedroom as I had done for the previous few days, unable to even make it out the door. Instead I staggered, drunk with sleep deprivation and distress, into 'Nanna's room', where my poor dad now slept among her things, her pillows laid down the side of the bed as if to make the shape of her. It's bad enough experiencing your own pain. But seeing the other people you love in pain too is brutal.

Her handbag was still on the floor by her side of the bed. I don't know why I thought I could do it then, but I sat down and opened it. It was like opening a memory box. All the things I knew would be in there were there. As familiar as my own. As familiar as Daisy now is with my things. I touched Mum's purse, her lipstick, her little wallet of photos which she constantly showed to friends and strangers alike, her comb, her tissues, her pen. Then I lifted out her notebook. Her neat handwriting waved at me like an old friend. She had taken her time to write just as she had taken her time to do most things: slowly and well. I just scrawled, perpetually and in perpetual motion, as my busy life dictated. Now, I flicked slowly through the pages. All the lists I expected were there: Christmas present lists, shopping lists, a recipe she must have written down from a friend, a list of clothes she was packing for a holiday. And then, there it was. A list I wasn't expecting. It simply said at the top: 'Things I Love About Alana'.

I think she must have written it earlier in the year for a compilation book my husband made for my fortieth birthday. But it had never made it into the book, Mum's self-deprecation and lack of confidence no doubt holding her back. And so it lay like a gift of love in her notebook. It was as if she had left me a message. Devastation made it beyond my ability to comprehend. I was learning to walk without the wheelchair but I didn't think the ground would ever be steady again, never knowing when the pillars of pressure from both ends of my life would fall in on top of me. How was I going to cope without her, bringing up my kids without directions and finding myself in the fog? But, as I realised that day reading my mum's list of things she loved about me best, the answers were in front of me. She had written that I was strong-willed and kind, determined and generous. And other things that will always make me smile. My mum had given me a map all my life and I just had to go back and learn how to read it.

Those first two weeks were a constant flip between love and loss. I would wake each morning with my newborn baby beside me, lifting her in to feed and cuddle her. My other girls would scamper into the room and we would all have a quick duvet snuggle before I got everyone dressed and gave them break-fast. I would keep my tears at bay and my face intact until I got Daisy delivered to school and Poppy to Montessori. Then, on the walk back home, with Ruby in the pram, I could let my tears and face fall.

I would try and figure out who I could get to look after Ruby so that I could go to visit Mum, then I would sit and feed my baby, taking in her smell and sucking in the feeling of love before heading to the hospital and entering that ward, where all I saw was horror and loss. There I would stay until it was time to rearrange my face again to collect the girls and make their tea. When they were asleep, Dad, Simon and I would sit quietly and try to figure out how to progress. But none of us had any idea. Every night my brother, Dad and I would regroup around my kitchen table, speaking small words into a space no words could fill, discussing what we would do if she died. Wondering what we would do if she didn't.

I would go to bed, crazed with lack of sleep, and breathe in the love and comfort of my girls. In the short bursts of sleep time between night-time feeds, I mostly lay awake, dazed with loss and fear.

The day my mother was moved back onto the open ward I knew we faced some decisions. It became clear my mum was no longer at risk of imminent death — but she had no risk of imminent life either. Suddenly we were in a situation which, despite our grief and shock, demanded we also deal with the issues of care. Mum was going to live. Now, as a family, we had to figure out how and where. I was just about able to manage my baby, children and Mum because she was in the hospital just up the road from my house. But then Dad said the words I had been dreading: 'I need to get back home.'

My dad had spent several weeks living in our house and he needed to get back to something resembling his own life. And with that, we realised, so did Mum. Simon, being the practical player of our party, took charge. 'I'll talk to the doctors about getting her transferred up to Belfast.'

It took another week but, eventually, she was taken by ambulance up the M1 on the journey I would now have to make repeatedly to visit her and support Dad. This was the right decision for my parents, but it presented me with a critical choice. How was I going to support them when I lived 200 kilometres away in Dublin? Now I had to start making challenging choices between my children and my parents.

3

Critical Choices

Our worst fear had been that Mum would die, but now we were faced with life, and it almost felt worse.

My lovely mum had recovered enough to avert death, but not enough to regain her life. If I thought it had been a challenge dividing my day between my mum in hospital, my newborn and my other children, it now felt catastrophic to have to figure out how to divide my week so I could care for them all.

It began the first weekend after Mum was transferred up to Belfast. I had to take my little girls to school and Montessori and say goodbye, knowing I wouldn't see them for three days. Daisy was still struggling to adapt to school and that Friday morning she clung to me, screaming at her classroom door, 'Please, Mummy, please don't go!'

'I'm so sorry, lovely, I have to go. Nanna is so sick, I have to see her. I'll be back soon,' I stammered as I hugged her hard.

But she clung so tight and cried so deep that the teacher had to pull her arms off me, and I had to leave the classroom while she was held back, her screams following me down the hallway. I managed to hold my face together until I dropped Poppy off at the next classroom where the Montessori was. Leaving her was equally traumatic, if not as dramatic. She just hung her head and nodded when I said goodbye and clung to me silently. I'm not sure which was worse.

I limped home, the pram holding me up, sobbing with the cruelty of the choices I had to make. I couldn't take them with me; Mum was in hospital and I had no-one to look after them up there. After feeding Ruby and packing up the car, I began that first awful two-and-a-half-hour drive up the M1. If I had known how many times I would make that journey, or for how many years, I'm not sure I'd have been able to leave my driveway that day.

In Belfast, Mum stayed in hospital for another couple of weeks, during which time I grieved and missed her back at home in Dublin, but I was finally able to spend time with my girls. Or I made the harrowing journey north, and grieved and missed them, while being horrified at who my mum had become.

Eventually, the decision was made for her to be released from hospital. It did not look likely that she would recover further. A critical choice had to be made. My mum needed twenty-four-hour care. The hospital had tried to give her some physiotherapy but she was now permanently paralysed down her right side, doubly incontinent and unable to feed herself — she was fed liquid nutrition through a tube in her stomach. She was brain damaged and confused. But she was still my mum.

She had begun to give us the occasional smile (albeit a little crooked) when she saw my dad, my brother and me. And Ruby. Her biggest smiles were for Ruby.

Dad was assessed by the health services and deemed fit and capable of looking after Mum at home, supported by a care package that included professional carers to come to the house to wash and change her regularly, throughout the day and night.

'I want to bring her home,' Dad said.

In one respect, we were all relieved. For Mum to be in the familiarity of her own home rather than among strangers in a care home was a huge comfort. And it meant I could bring my girls up with me and we could all relax in the family house with Mum rather than have to visit her in a home.

'But, Dad, it's a huge responsibility for you,' my brother said gently. My dad was an outdoors man. At seventy-four he still went running three times a week, and climbed mountains. Now he faced being house-bound.

'Dad, you won't have to do this on your own,' I said. 'Simon and I will be here as much as we can, but the burden will still very much fall on you.'

'I'll give it a go,' he said in his forthright, practical way.

'OK,' we agreed. 'But there is no expectation on you. If you get to the point where you feel you can't do it, that's OK. We'll think of something else.'

And so, with that decision made, my mum was brought home, and my dad became a full-time carer.

Simon and I sat with the calendar and divided up our weekend support for the next few months. He lived in Edinburgh, I lived in Dublin, and we both had families with small children in school, so weekends were the only real option for us to help. We had to give up family time with our new families to give family time for our old family, there was no getting around that.

That first weekend we got Mum home, and her new specialised bed (with sides that came up and a pressure mattress that moved constantly) was installed downstairs in the old dining room, I knew we were in this as a family. But driving away from Dad waving in the doorway, leaving him to care for her alone, it didn't feel like it at all. Guilt strapped himself in beside me in the passenger seat and tortured me all the way home.

★   ★   ★

In those first few weeks, there were lots of tough practical choices to make. But once they'd been made, they were done. It was the constant emotional choices that had to be made that would make the next few years so challenging.

The pain of the thought of my mum dying was extraordinary. But the pain of the thought of her living like this was worse. The immediate role reversal, of child to parent, was in stark contrast to my new role as parent to children and new baby. And, at times, the push and pull of those two ends of my life threatened to tear me to shreds. A stroke — like many other catastrophic conditions such as Alzheimer's or dementia — is like an earthquake. A seismic shift that leaves an altered landscape and your foundations rocked to their core. When you come out to assess the damage, every fearful step is on unknown, shaken ground.

Like many women, I went into parenting still expecting to be parented. Mum was a huge help to me with my first two children. She would come down on the Belfast-Dublin train, and while I was now responsible for lots of people, I always remained her responsibility. She would force me to slow down, to sit down and have a chat over the teapot. She would busy herself with all those little jobs that were just one job too many for a busy mum — scrubbing down the hardened baby food mulch on the dining table chairs, giving the cooker top a good scrub to remove the caked-on burned spills, tidying up the drawers and dressers and generally Mary Poppinsing my life a little bit. She was present at every one of my girls' birthdays, there in the background of every video with a cloth in her hand, wiping up spills and lapping up the thrills of being so involved with my family life.

And so, even though she was slowing down a bit, my expectation was she would be around to help out when Ruby was born. Her most important role of course was to make me sit down and have a cup of tea. Instead, I had to hold the thickened tea to her lips and help her drink hers. I faced not only parenting without her support, but also having to care for her and my dad too.

My oldest child had just started school and was still crying going into class each morning. She needed her mum.

My middle child had just started Montessori and was bursting with new knowledge and stories for me to hear. She needed her mum.

My newest child had just started life. She *really* needed her mum.

My mum was dying. I needed my mum. And she needed me.

The tug of love played out a tug of war on my heart.

★ ★ ★

As my new reality began to sink in, there was a moment I thought about often. A realisation I had when I returned home from the hospital the morning after Mum's stroke. After I'd packed Mum's bag, I went downstairs to see the girls before I headed straight back to the hospital. As I entered the kitchen, I realised with a jolt that I couldn't bring Ruby with me. She wasn't allowed on the ward. No children were. The shock of what this was going to mean prickled my skin with tiny needles of realisation. As time went on, the choices I had to make would build and build until I felt I was being stabbed over and over and over by the knives of guilt.

I wanted to breastfeed Ruby. I had breastfed the others and slowly, from a few weeks, had introduced breast-pumped bottles so that their dad could feed them and enjoy the bond (and frankly allow me to sleep). But for the first few weeks, it was important to get the milk supply right. During her first feed, Ruby had latched on with the intensity she would bring to life every day, and we had been good to go from the start.

It had taken Daisy and me a month, support groups, nipple guards and two doses of mastitis before we got our milk quota right. Eighteen months later Poppy arrived and feeding *her* was like some sort of grotesque TV Wild Woman challenge, trying to keep my nipples in Poppy's mouth while Daisy lay on the back of the sofa (literally) strangling me. This time was going to be different. This time, I would breastfeed in peace while the girls were at school, under the canopy of pink bunting, and that filtered music would be playing, and George Clooney would stick his head around the door and offer to take out the nappy bin for me. Mum would visit and we would drink Earl Grey and eat a little bit of something nice and all would be good with the world.

But life had other plans. George hadn't appeared, and my mum was in a different place entirely.

On that first morning, I had wanted to breastfeed my newborn baby but my mum was lying, dying, in hospital and I needed to be there. My baby couldn't be there. Yet my baby needed feeding every three hours. The shock and awfulness of what was to become a classic Sandwich Years conundrum was as devastating as Mum's stroke. My husband gave me the look that said, *I've something to say you won't like.*

He came right out with it. 'Will I go and get the pump?'

While he got the pump from the attic, I held my little baby girl, her eyes dark pools of wonder gazing up at me. But instead of suckling the milk from my breast, our bodies warming each other's skin, her eyes locked on mine, her fingers wrapped around one of mine, her mammary meal would be delivered via pumping paraphernalia that sounded like a life-support machine and looked like a grotesque torture appliance. I sat on the sofa, two pumps attached to my breasts, my other daughters slightly alarmed that Mummy was being milked.

And so I pumped out my milk, and handed over my baby, and left my new family that needed me, to be with my old family who needed me more. I touched my Caesarean wound. It was only flesh-deep, yet I felt I had been cut in two.

Over that first week, I would sit by Mum's side, trying to read her eyes, and then I'd walk out the front door of the hospital where my husband or one of my friends would be looking after Ruby. I would cuddle her, squeeze her to me, breathing away death and sucking in life. I would try to rub my skin on her so she remembered my scent. I would talk to my girls on the phone and try to keep my voice straight as one of my daughters cried that she wanted me. Then I would feed Ruby in my friend's car or my husband's car, sobbing as she gulped, and then they would take her away again and I would walk back down that corridor in St James's, my heart wrung out with the stress of abandoning the people who needed me most, to sit with the person abandoning me, who I needed most.

One day, I had thrown up right there on the floor of the main crowded foyer, a vomit made up of tears and blood and trauma and shock, my body heaving out the pain that had been sitting in my stomach. But as I'd staggered away towards the stroke unit, apologising profusely to the cleaner, I realised it was just my lunch. The pain was still there.

Now that my mum was settled back at home in Belfast, she needed caring almost in the same way as my baby did. And so began our new situation. I would drive up the two-and-a-half-hour-long motorway from Dublin to Belfast. Sometimes I took the girls with me, unable to be separated from them again. But that brought its own challenges. In Belfast, my mum was bed-bound, so I was house-bound, and entertaining three small people in a small room was tantamount to being tied and gagged and tortured with hot pokers. If they stayed in Dublin, they got to spend time with their dad who worked such long hours during the week, and obviously wanted his time with them at the weekends. So, that meant taking the girls to school on a Friday morning and saying goodbye amidst tears and regret. Guilt always walked home beside me, prodding me with bony fingers. I would then feed Ruby, pack the car and make the long, lonely journey up the motorway, hoping I would get there before Ruby woke up, although I often had to pull into a busy motorway lay-by to feed her in the front seat. Sometimes, that was a blessing, as my eyes needed to close for a moment.

The sleep deprivation and exhaustion of a

new baby meant that the constant driving up and down that motorway was often danger-ous, the pull of my eyes to close competing with the pull of the road in front. The weather that winter made it treacherous.

Over those first awful months, Ireland experienced one of its worst snow and ice periods for a long time, with the coldest November on record. I drove through so many snow and sleet storms that I felt like I was driving through a grey-and-white tunnel for two-and-a-half hours. I couldn't even play music in case it disturbed the sleeping Ruby. I would often arrive with my hands frozen in such a focused fist around the steering wheel that it took a moment for me to unclench them.

This drive, though, gave me time to think, to be alone with my thoughts. Often, by the time I rounded the last corner before my mum and dad's house, I would have to pull over, wipe away my tear-smudged makeup, put on my lipstick and rearrange my face, before I drove into their driveway and hooted my horn in 'Hello!'. I would then check in with the childminder who we had hired to look after the girls until my husband could rush home from work. Naturally, the choices didn't just affect me and my brother. They affected our partners, who had to take up the extra burden of childcare to enable us to parent-care. Those weekends were a torrent of pain and grief. I cried all the way up that motorway at leaving behind my girls and husband, and I cried all the way down that motorway at leaving behind my mum.

I constantly memorised every 'last' situation with my mum — her last kiss to me as she said goodbye after visiting me in hospital with Ruby; our last phone call just a couple of hours before her catastrophic stroke, how happy she'd been; our last hug; our last fight. Everyday moments in our relationship, now forever memorised as momentous. And, alongside that, I thought of all my new firsts with Ruby. Her first smile, like a rainbow after a storm. Her first giggle, a trickle that gushed into a flood. Her first spoonful of solid food — her surprise, my delight, her excitement, my satisfaction, from those first tentative tastes of rice, to the bags of heart-shaped cubes of steamed sweet potato, broccoli, carrot, pear and apple that burst from my freezer. And for that first year, the parallels of caring for a baby and a parent could not have been more pronounced. I would wake up every other weekend in Mum and Dad's house, Ruby asleep in the carrycot beside me. I would gaze into her sleepy little eyes and stroke her face, thrilled with her recognition. Then I would pass Mum's old bedroom that she would never see again, and go downstairs. I would gaze into her sleepy old eyes and stroke her face, thrilled with any recognition.

I would lay Ruby out on the changing mat, and lift out a nappy and change her, always keeping eye contact. Then I would lay out my mum's nappy. They call them pads to protect everyone's dignity, but they are nonetheless nappies. Big, oversized adult nappies. To see the glamorous, living, loving woman you grew up with reduced to wearing a nappy, and knowing she is aware of it, is a feeling that I can't describe. So I won't try. If childbirth takes away some dignity, then old age takes away all of it. Then, with Ruby changed, I would either wait for the carers to come and change Mum, or try and wipe up the mess that had come out during the night, deliberately avoiding eye contact. Then I would make breakfast.

That first meal of the day was no longer a solitary, self-indulgent affair where I would pile my Special K high and top with raspberries (or indulge in toast and chocolate spread and a nice cup of tea). This was now a three-way spoon sprint. With Ruby sitting in her high chair and Mum's bedhead raised I would turn to my right and spoon a mouthful of porridge into my baby, turn to my left and spoon a mouthful into my mum, and finally turn to my bowl and feed myself. One for Ruby, one for Mum, one for me. Sandwiched in the middle.

I spoonfed my mum — favourite flavours no longer lighting up her eyes — and I spoonfed my new baby, marvellous mouthfuls of taste surprising and lighting up her face. Many a time they both spat out their food, and I would try not to cry with the frustration.

I would rub cream on Ruby's chubby little kicking legs, and massage cream into Mum's thinning, useless legs. Mum could now drink proper unthickened tea so I would give her a cup of cooled tea in a plastic sippy cup with a spout and handles, and give milk to Ruby in a similar one. Mum even had a baby monitor beside her bed which was connected to another upstairs in Dad's room (or mine when he was away).

The brutality of it haunts me still.

The awe I felt for Ruby was matched by the shock of Mum's sudden demise — two ends of my emotional spectrum, my mum and my baby — and the powerlessness of the situation nearly struck me down as swiftly as my mum's stroke had struck her.

It wasn't just my mum and baby that

compounded these feelings. The awe I felt for Ruby was the same as it had been for my first two girls and it is something that has never waned. I still catch myself staring at them, breathless at their beauty and vibrancy, wondering how I made them. And their need was great too. They had entered the most special times of their lives to date, leaving the security of the world I had created for them at home, to start exploring the world I had gently pushed them towards at school, and they needed me to be there.

But there were so many times when I couldn't be there because I was with Mum. And then when I was home with them, catching up on our precious time, and I would hear the strain in Dad's voice when something distressing had happened and I knew I should be there with him. In those early days of settling into a new life with Mum in bed and Dad her carer, every little new step — every explosive bowel movement, every vomit, every little thing — was a huge thing. It was all new, and none of us knew what to do. My husband worked long hours and now had to take up the slack of childcare. At some point in the future, I knew I would have to think about going back to work again as a freelance charity consultant. In those first few months, every which way I turned, somebody needed me, and I couldn't be everywhere. I couldn't be there for them all. It felt as though I was failing everyone at a time that they needed me most. There was no filter music, no George. Just me, and it was a very lonely place to be.

★ ★ ★

While my life took on this new relay of responsibility, of facing constant critical choices between my children and my parents, I also began to question the critical choices I had made in my thirties that led to this perfect storm of care — young children and elderly parents.

I had come late to the parenting party. Or so I was told. I was thirty-five years old when I got pregnant the first time. And I was being told left, right and centre that thirty-five was the new twenty-five. It seems my eggs didn't get the memo. I had been busy living and travelling and careering and I'd had no desire to get proactive about parenting before that. Instead of nurturing babies, I had nurtured my career. I had always loved writing, and I was also interested in world issues. In fact, for most of my early adult years I'd wanted to be Kate Adie, the BBC foreign correspondent. And it wasn't just because of her array of khaki trousers. Having studied English and International Politics at university, I had spent a few years building up my skills in communications roles in London in between bursts of travelling. It was on one of these bursts — a volunteer job as communications officer on a Raleigh International expedition to Borneo — that I met my husband-to-be.

I was twenty-six. Amid the rainforests and mountains of southeast Asia I fell in love, and not just with the brown-eyed, red-haired orangutans. There was a brown-eyed, red-haired doctor too. He was also a volunteer on the expedition, and our romance was intense. Eventually, he returned back to his home and job in the UK and I kept travelling and our romance fizzled out. But a few years later, it was rekindled and this time, we settled in Dublin and got married.

When I got my dream job with UNICEF Ireland I got to combine my passion for writing and humanitarian issues, and to start forging the career I wanted. For five amazing years, this job was my priority. I had the privilege of meeting incredible people in countries like Iraq and Sierra Leone, people who really showed me what strength looked like in times of extreme stress and upheaval. I went on to become Fundraising and Communications Director of the children's charity

Barnardo's and it was only at this stage that I felt ready to begin my own family.

At first, it had seemed so easy. I got pregnant straight away and, before long, I had had two beautiful girls. Emergency C-sections, mastitis and nipple guards notwithstanding, my foray into family-making had gone quite well. So when I got pregnant in an embarrassingly short time after Poppy was born, I was shocked and excited. As I trawled the internet for a triple buggy (yes, I was facing three babies under three and a half), my mum looked at me with a pained expression, her eyebrows raised. I knew things were serious when both eyebrows communicated with me. They said something along the lines of, *Are you out of your mind? Have you no self-control? This is what happens when you leave it all so late. Well, it's your decision, don't come crying to me when you're up to your neck in nappies and bottles.*

My rolled eyes would communicate back, *Yes, well, that's all very helpful but it is what it is, so please will you get on with my ironing while I stock the fridge with broccoli purée.* Sometimes, Mum and I could have entire conversations without speaking.

So on my third pregnancy, when I went for my first scan, walking down the same corridor that I had walked so many times before to see the two previous pink prawns in my belly, I felt no fear. I knew that approaching forty, I was pushing the parental boundaries of age but that was just magazine talk. I'm no statistic. I lay on the bed and the doctor put the gel on my belly. I couldn't wait to see my new prawn. The doctor stopped smiling. He kept his eyes focused on the scan, and I searched it for my baby. I was never able to read the screens. But I could read his face. It was solemn, and quiet. 'I'm sorry,' he said. 'There is no heartbeat.'

I had become a statistic. One in five pregnancies end in miscarriage. This is a fact. But it's also a reality for so many women, and it hurts. Statistics never tell the stories of pain. They are numbers, but these are hearts. Hearts no longer beating. I went on to have three more miscarriages. Four devastating losses in total, four babies I carried inside me for varying lengths of time, but never held. And so my mum had held me instead. I desperately wanted another baby but had discovered it was a chromosomal anomaly that had caused my losses. Would I ever be able to have my longed-for child, especially now I was pushing forty?

Somehow, in the chaos of my chromosomes, two miracle girls had emerged in a statistically sinister environment where the odds were not stacked in their favour.

My mum had nagged me constantly during my twenties and early thirties. 'If you don't hurry up, I'll end up a Zimmer Frame Granny!' she would say. And as I started to navigate the wave of friends' frustrations and disappointments, as well as my own, I began to wonder if I would be a Zimmer Frame Mummy as well. (There were definitely times during the Double Buggy years of two babies under two that I felt that way.)

In the end, my mum was never a Zimmer Frame Granny. For five years she was a Granny with Gusto, a Ninja Nanna. But just days after Ruby came along, near to my forty-first birthday, my mum couldn't even use a Zimmer frame. She had become a Non-existent Nanna, lying in a bed dazed while her grandchildren grew up, amazed. And my feelings of loss were not just for me, but for my daughters. With one stroke, my girls had lost the most important person in their lives, apart from me and their dad.

Before Mum's stroke, I would often wonder what might have been if I had started my family earlier. But mostly I had pushed those thoughts aside as I accounted for every year of travelling, career-building, party-pleasing as one I would not have given up. But the legacy of that is increasingly being seen. As more women of my generation face into the Sandwich Years when delayed parenting collides with caring for parents, I wonder what I will be advising my girls. What will I tell them? Will I tell them to try for families earlier? I don't know, but I will ask them to think about the consequences of whatever choices they make. As I struggled under the pressure of the Sandwich Years, I wondered about the price I might be paying.

I'm sure that in the folklore of family heritage, when someone wants to have a baby they simply close their eyes, think of their respective country and hey presto, nine months later they are up to their armpits in interfering mothers-in-law, sore nipples and buckets of rancid nappies.

I had lived a life of adventure, but now my life would be dominated by misfortune. I was one of the new feminist statistics — pregnant at forty, exhaustedly extolling the virtues of late parenthood as I brought up two toddlers with no surrounding extended family, while secretly wishing I was actually ten years younger (rather than just wishing I looked ten years younger). I also played perfectly into the fearful facts of delayed reproduction by having four miscarriages in seven pregnancies, my grief and loss hidden behind the commonness of my experiences. Many of my peers, from my closest buddies to my wider network of friends and acquaintances, all seemed to be having a challenging time getting or remaining pregnant. We were feminists still fighting for our place in society but, now, we were also fighting for our place as mothers. Infertility. Miscarriage. Chromosomal issues. Unexplained problems. A few decades and generations before, it appeared (on the surface at least) that childbirth was all about cross-stitched gifts and congratulations, but with my generation of late-blooming boomers, it seemed more about crossed fingers and commiserations.

In recent years, it seems to have become much more complicated. While my peers and I rode on the shoulders of our forbearing feminist barrier-breakers, we travelled the world, climbed the corporate ladder and took our rightful place on a bar stool. However, as we looked down from those dizzying heights, we were, and are, increasingly finding ourselves struggling not only to cope with pregnancy and parenting at the tail end of our bodies' best breeding window, but struggling to cope with becoming pregnant at all. Feminist advances have enabled us to make choices about when we start a family. But sometimes nature then takes that choice away. We could suddenly gamble with nature, play reproduction roulette.

As I write this book, the news has been full of 'extreme' older mother cases, including the story of a sixty-seven-year-old who gave birth to twins. But, sensational headlines aside, there has been a steady and significant increase in the rate of 'older' mothers giving birth over the past ten years. According to the Central Statistics Office the average age of mothers giving birth increased from 30.3 years in 2001 to 31.5 years in 2010 and the age of first time mothers rose from 28.8 years in 2006 to 29.4 years in 2010.[1] In fact, there are now more first-time mothers in the thirty to thirty-four age bracket than in the twenty-five to twenty-nine age group, and there is a 50 per cent increase in women over forty having babies compared to just a decade ago. And 2014 became the first year ever recorded in the UK in which more women over the age of thirty-five gave birth than women under the age of twenty-five.[2] In Ireland, according to an ESRI Report in 2012, more than half of all first-time mothers were in their thirties with a quarter of all births to women aged thirty-five and over.[3] There are lots of reasons for this. Our suffragette sisters helped us look up from the kitchen floor towards the ceiling and our career opportunities took off. The trend towards later maternity is strongest among women with better education and qualifications, so delaying pregnancy to develop a career, travel or build up financial security has become common and an important part of our right to choose. Also, as divorce rates increase, so second families abound. Many women delay having children because they are not at the right time of their lives; they want to strive to achieve other things first, or sometimes circumstances delay them.

So Ruby was hard fought for. There had been so much grief and loss before she was born. We rolled the dice one more time, and finally threw a winning hand. This made the grief and loss of Mum's stroke so soon after her birth much harder to deal with.

Mum lay in bed, trapped in her body, confused by her thoughts. I still had her, but I'd lost her guidance, her support, her love, her ability to walk into my house and see the pile of ironing and slightly rearrange the cushions; the person who was teaching me to be a mother.

What devastated me more than anything now that I'd lost my best supporter was the realisation that *I* was no longer invincible. That I might not be around when my girls needed *me* most. That realisation was hard to take — even if my youngest daughter waits until she is thirty (which is early by modern standards) to start a family, I will be seventy. If she waits until she is forty like I did, I will be eighty. Will I be around when she needs me most? Is one of the legacies of feminism a generation of women facing their most challenging years alone?

I would look at my mum and then look at Ruby. When I thought about all the dramas I've had in my life, I would think, *Will I be around for hers?* If she needs me to help her through the possible grief and upsets of fertility issues. When she needs me to hold her hand through her first pregnancy and clean her cooker top (if I ever get a handle on that one). When she needs me to tell her that her baby is the most beautiful child in the world and that she is the best mum. To babysit, to listen, to counsel, to share her joy, and share the burden. Will I be there? Will I be able? *Why did I wait so long?* I thought I had to live my life before I had children . . . that children somehow represented the end of something. I never realised, of course, that they were the beginning. Guilt didn't just accompany me on my trips to Belfast or my weekends at home. Guilt came to bed with me at night and whispered words of worry in my ear. Why did I waste so much time? Why didn't I give my mum many more years to enjoy her grandchildren? Why did I deprive my children of her?

I had no answers to these questions. Life doesn't come pre-planned and stuff happens that we can't control. I had to accept and be happy with the choices I had made — all that travelling, all those adventures had made me the person, and mother, I am. All we can do is make our choices, and live with them the best way we can. But I do believe society has to wake up to the fact that we are living longer and giving life later and, because of this, there could be a generation left with little or no family support — no support systems, no guidance and no energy with which to help raise their children.

My life used to be simple. Clear-cut. Our roles were defined and refined. We all knew where we stood. My mum was my mum. I was her daughter. She annoyed me and I annoyed her, but she loved me and cared for me a lot. I loved her back and cared for her a little. Then I became a mum and I had daughters and the cycle began again. So far, so simple. Now the roles were blurred, the lines in the sand rolled over by the waves of catastrophe and stress. Now, my mum no longer looked after me at all. I looked after her a lot.

As, six months later, that awful first winter

brightened at last with the promise of colour from spring flowers, Mum began to talk a little more. I brushed her hair and put on her makeup. I did her nails and rubbed cream on her skin. I cleaned her house and laid out her clothes. I also looked after my daughters, brushed their hair, hid my makeup from them. I read them stories, and put plasters on their bruised knees. I fed them and laid out their clothes. But the angst of my mum's demise, and the sleep-deprived stress of a young baby overwhelmed me. Daisy called me 'Grumpy Mummy'.

'I'm not grumpy all the time,' I insisted, but she gave me that look that only children can give. The look that says, *Yes, but it's the grumpy times that count*.

Sometimes, my children and I can have whole conversations without speaking.

There is no rewind in parenting. No pause button. In those first few months, there was no time for me to stop parenting my girls so I could parent my mum, and then get back to them. No time for me to pause on Mum, so I could raise my new baby and give her all the love she needed. No time to pause on Ruby and Mum, so I could sit and listen to the chitter and chatter of my girls living their lives. I was sandwiched in a vortex of dependence and there was no-one else to step up to the plate but me. There is no rewind, and no fast-forward. The only button to push is play and the only thing is to live through the moment. And no-one was going to soften the blow. Certainly not my children.

I remember being in one of my usual get-out-of-the-house-with-two-children-and-a-baby-dressed-fed-and-somewhat-intact-by-half-eight-in-the-morning modes when the final hurdle of getting laced runners on Daisy's feet was a hurdle too far. I lost the plot and threw a tantrum — it was quite impressive too. At one point the runners were hurled across the room. I am not proud of these moments. I am not proud at all, but sometimes, just sometimes, hurling a shoe across the floor is the only way to step into the next minute. It was a choice between hurl the shoe across the room or hurl myself on the floor and cry.

Eventually, I strapped everyone into the car, took a deep breath and sheepishly apologised for my outburst. 'It's just hard,' I explained, 'getting everyone out in the mornings with no help from anyone.' Daisy just looked at me — not unlike my mother used to, it has to be said, when she was making an annoyingly accurate point. It's amazing how much one raised eyebrow can say. Her voice was aloof. 'Yes, Mummy, but we are the little people, and you are the big person.'

Ouch.

Ouch, but true. I *was* the big person and suddenly there was no other bigger person above me. The buck stopped with me. No matter where the lines are, or what the roles are, or even if I have no idea where I stand anymore, I was the big person. Parenting my mother, being parented by my child. Lines blurred indeed.

4

Becoming a Carer

We can all make plans and follow dreams. But so much in our lives is out of our hands. We think we are in control, but life always has the upper hand and we never know when or how it will play its cards.

Finding myself in the Sandwich Years was a shock. But even without the pressure of raising children, learning to care for a parent can be deeply challenging and when life hands us that card, we just have to learn to play it. Nobody can really plan for it, and perhaps because it's not even a topic generally discussed, we are not prepared for it. Yet for thousands of people, caring for a parent has become a reality. We have a vague idea how to care for a baby and growing children (although I'm not sure I have ever felt fully in charge of that) but learning to care for a parent isn't something many of us have any idea about.

When you have a baby you can go to breastfeeding groups and bond with your nipples, or toddler groups so other children can bond with your nippers. You can bring your child on a play date so they can play and you can drink tea with the mum. (Or wine, depending how the day has gone. There are just days when it is always wine o'clock.)

Caring for a parent, you are on your own.

Their teeth fall out, their toes merge in thickened skin, their scalp starts to flake, all manner of untold issues you can't just go down to the Aged Parent Group and ask about, over a cup of stewed tea and a plate of soft biscuits.

That fateful night I walked through the door of the St James's Hospital A&E, I walked into a completely different life. Where was the colour-coded chart? Where was the handbook? Overnight, I went from having a mother who cared for me, to a mother who needed my care. At first, I was rendered almost incapable. I had worked in war zones, travelling to Iraq when Saddam Hussein was still in charge, interviewing child soldiers and girl sex slaves in Sierra Leone. I had run busy departments, travelled around the world, but this was beyond my capacity. It was just too much to handle. Too much need, too much grief, too much responsibility. Both ends of my candle were burning (and I wasn't even going out) and I was just waiting for the flames to engulf me. The initial grief had been over Mum dying. Now our grief was that she might live like this for years. Very quickly, my family and I had had to learn how to care for someone who needed twenty-four-hour help.

She could do nothing for herself. The few months of physiotherapy had failed to restore any use in her arm or leg, although her speech was coming back. Now we had to support Dad caring for Mum at home, supported by a significant community care package. Thankfully, my dad is a highly practical man which helps in a situation like this, and he took the brunt of the care. He is one of those people who is just able to do things. A writer and journalist, he taught himself photography and in his retirement has produced several beautiful coffee-table books on local landscapes; he wood-turns and makes furniture; has produced gallons of (undrinkable!) wine, grows fruit and vegetables and makes his own soups.

After Mum was released from hospital, Dad converted the downstairs dining room into a bedroom lounge for both of them, where Mum could lie in a specialised bed that had a constantly moving air mattress, and Dad could sit in his big black leather chair so they could be together in the evening to watch TV.

At first, Mum couldn't eat real food and so had to be fed via a tube through her stomach. Every night Dad had to hook up the bag of liquid and plug it into a little device inserted in her stomach. Caring for someone who is completely dependent is not for the faint-hearted. He made shelves for the feeding pump, and bought drawers for all her nighties. He made ramps to get her wheelchair in and out of the house, and constructed a pully drying system to keep on top of all the sheets and nighties she went through.

She would never climb the stairs again into her bedroom. Never clean or cook in her kitchen. But she was in her home, in a pressure bed, occasionally hoisted into a wheelchair so she could sit in the kitchen. And with that decision, my seventy-four-year-old dad who had spent his life walking the hills, climbing mountains, running marathons and keeping constantly busy became a full-time carer, and as housebound as my mum had become bed-bound.

When a parent has a stroke, or any other devastating illness or condition, it strikes at the heart of everyone they care about, and everyone becomes involved in their care. We were told that the first twenty-four hours are critical. But the situation isn't over in twenty-four hours. Sometimes it remains critical for years.

'Carer' refers to someone who is family or professional, who will look after the needs of someone else. But 'care' means so much more than this. It is loaded with practical implications, from making sure someone has their shopping and meals, to feeding that person and keeping them alive. It could mean helping to clean their house, and being responsible for cleaning their bodies, teeth, hair, ears and mouth, every day. It can mean arranging care to ensure they are fed, washed and changed, sourcing help and managing many aspects of their life including financial, legal and practical, as well as being a full-time nurse. It means being responsible emotionally as well as physically for someone you love. Worry, anxiety, fear, grief and guilt are all best buddies, and they move in with you. And for many of us Sandwich Generationers, and those without children who must care for their parents, it is almost impossible to be prepared. The practical implications alone are vast.

It can be the wrangle of websites that jangle the most organised of people. My dad's kitchen became filled with piles of paper, forms and leaflets to wade through. He actually gave up on the thirty-page document he needed to complete to apply for power of attorney for my mum. Never mind being a full-time carer, it was a full time job working out how to fill out the forms to become a full-time carer.

My family happens to be fairly practical so we had a clear idea of what Mum would have wanted, and Dad had already put all his papers in order and given my brother and me details of all his codes, accounts and financial information, so that we would never be left struggling to work things out if something happened to him. We have since agreed that my brother would have power of attorney over my dad, should he ever start being unable to make decisions.

These might seem like difficult conversations, but consider the statistics: with three in five people becoming a carer at some point in their lives, they are conversations that need to be had. There are an estimated 187,112 family carers in Ireland (over 6.5 million in the UK) and the number is on the rise (it is expected to increase by 28 per cent by 2021).[4]

The majority of these carers are women, the majority are married, and aged between forty-five and sixty-five. As a society, do we talk about death enough? It's such an important part of life, yet it can still be a taboo subject. Ireland's ageing population (in parallel with most European countries and the US) represents a real challenge for governments, communities and families to ensure systems and supports are in place, not only for those needing care but for the carers. Dealing with the care of our parents should begin, in theory anyway, long before they start to need that support.

Before Mum's stroke, Simon and I had started to think about the practicalities of our parents' old age as an abstract notion. For Dad's seventieth birthday we rented a beautiful house in the Loire Valley in France. After an evening of cards and wine, my parents went to bed first, and the rest of us 'young ones' (all past or pushing forty) slunk off like teenagers to have another cheeky bottle of red. Mum's arthritis was getting worse, and we had conversations about how we could persuade our parents to adapt their house to make it easier for her. We had no notion of what was to come but, on one of those evenings, we came up with a plan to convince them to take out an equity release loan. The bank would give them a loan that would be paid back from the eventual sale of their house when they died. Over the next year, they extended and widened their kitchen and put in a downstairs bathroom 'just in case' Mum's bad knees couldn't get her up the stairs. But adapting the house meant that when we had to start making decisions around her care after she had her stroke, we had the option of keeping her at home.

Adjusting to the role reversal can be very stressful. But there are people there to help with the practical elements. Learning how to care for a parent cannot be done alone and if you are caring for a loved one at home there are organisations that will provide guidance and practical support. Our family and friends gathered around her as we all tried to make her life worth living. But others came too, a whole community of people who contributed and gave support. The carers, who are professional in all the practical aspects of the care that we were just learning about, came into my mum and dad's house five or six times a day. They even let themselves in at 3 a.m. to change her pad. And while my dad had become a full-time carer and my brother and I had become part-time carers, we could not do any of it without the (mostly) women who come to our house day in, day out.

It is one of the most challenging jobs I can imagine. The intimacy of cleaning and washing and wiping up the messes, with as much love and care as if they were their own family is heroic. They are heroes. Unsung and underpaid. Many of them became a regular part of our lives. Many of them, who have grown to love my mum, didn't just bring their practical support, they brought emotional support too. They brought smiles, and 'Hello gorgeous', to my mum. They noticed every time I did her makeup and told my mum how lovely she looked.

I talked to them and heard their stories.

They dealt with every scenario you could imagine regarding the care of dependent people. And many you couldn't. They told me about old people being left alone all day, and that the carers were the only company they had. They also told me of young people who had been injured in accidents who, like my mum, needed twenty-four-hour support. They brought a cheery face to my dad on tough days and they looked out for him too.

There was one really cheerful carer, Teri, who always lifted our spirits. I asked her once why she did it. It seemed such a shocking job as I came to terms with some of its more challenging aspects. But Teri just looked at me in surprise. 'I love my job,' she said. 'I love caring.'

She told me how often she would stay late with old ladies who live on their own. She gave extra time to chat to old men who had no-one else to talk to. Individuals like Teri provide comfort to families who are shellshocked and grief-stricken. They give the family a hug as well as the patient. For many I have met, it is a vocation. These are the people that enable our loved ones to be cared for in the comfort of their own homes, or in a home from home. Mum had several respite stays in a care home and I have nothing but praise for the people who looked after her. Without that community care, she would have had to go into a nursing home. Ireland, like the UK and other European countries, is striving to develop the necessary community care for the elderly with a policy focused on keeping older people in their homes for as long as possible. But we are still playing catch-up. The cost of developing coordinated care-based community supports far outweigh the cost of caring for elderly people in care homes and hospital, and progress is finally being made here to enable our elderly people to be cared for as much as possible in the comfort of their own homes. There is a variety of home help packages that include nursing and therapy services, respite care and, in 2015, new extensive home-care packages were made more available, but it varies from region to region and families must research options.

There is other support out there. Both Ireland and the UK have carers' associations that will provide practical guidance and help, and a number of charities for the care of elderly people also give support and information. At the back of the book, I've included websites which we found useful over the past years.

★   ★   ★

The practical and physical implications of caring for a parent are considerable. Feeding your mother. Changing your father. But the emotional cost cannot be counted. A gut-wrenching, heart-squeezing, life-sucking situation you cannot escape from. Seeing them in pain. Realising their mortality. Feeling guilty about not doing enough. Feeling stressed from doing too much. These are the people who have got you through life, and now you have to see them through to death. If you think there is nothing more frustrating than a child refusing to eat the lovingly made organic mulch you've prepared them, just wait until your parent clamps their mouth and refuses to eat.

There is a silver lining too of course. You get to care for the person who has cared so much for you. You get to help them through indignity and loss. You get to keep that connection. For me, caring drew our family together. But it is one of the hardest challenges many of us will face.

I still remember the shock when I first became a mother, and the sheer workload of caring for an infant. How defenceless an infant is and how much bodily fluid they produce. I remember in those early Double Buggy years when Daisy was a wobbler and Poppy was a baby the sheer amount of poo, vomit, wee and disgusting jobs that became the everyday norm. There are the worms, the lice, the diarrhoea, the regurgitation, and the snot. Then there is the category labelled 'projectile'. Projectile vomit is one of those moments you wish you had narcolepsy so you could wake up when the whole thing is over and cleared up. This is especially true when they do it in the car and it goes everywhere, including down the back of your neck and in your hair. Projectile diarrhoea is an art to behold. My all-time favourite was chasing a diarrhoea-spilling child up the stairs to the toilet, and tripping so that I fell face down in a trail of yellow shit. During my thirty-five pre-motherhood years, the worst I had ever had to wipe up was cat poo when I locked my kitten in the house one day. Within three years of having babies, I was swimming in shit and awash in vomit. But I had sort of expected this. Nothing prepares you for having to cope when the person vomiting and shitting is your parent.

That first year after my mum's stroke, I felt like an inhuman amount of my time was spent up to my armpits in other people's bodily excrement. Many stroke patients have no control over their bodily functions. When my mum needed to go, she went. Often it would be some time before the carers were due to come and change her.

It took two people to change my mum. Being paralysed meant she was a dead weight and rolling and holding her in position required two trained people who knew what they were doing. This meant she would have to lie in her own mess for however long it took the carers to arrive. If this was a terrible thing for me and the rest of my family to endure, it was so much worse for her. Her anguished eyes spoke to me again, and they told me she was embarrassed and ashamed and she hated being this way.

As her speech improved she would often say 'I hate this.' She couldn't ask questions or have a proper conversation, but she could tell me that she hated this situation. Confused, sometimes she got curious and put her one moving appendage — her left hand — down the bed to check things out. Sometimes her hand would come back up covered in whatever was down there, and she'd end up smearing it over her face or through her hair.

She was forever pulling open the pads. It was one of the most stressful aspects of dealing with our new situation. I had to clean her teeth, pick out the dirt from her nails, and perform all sorts of basic care that she could no longer do for herself. At times it took every fibre of my being to not gag, not to scrunch my face.

I would remember how I used to sit as a child on her bed, transfixed as I watched her reflection in the mirror, as she sat at the dressing table and put on her makeup. She would say she was 'putting on her face'. Now, forty years later, I knew I had to put on mine so that she would never know this was anything but the most lovely of jobs.

Whatever about my dignity, Mum's had been stripped away. She had strangers doing the most intimate of tasks, cleaning and washing her. She had her husband or daughter wiping up overspill from the pad to keep her comfortable until the carers came. My dad did this far more than anyone — and he had the sheets and night clothes to contend with too. Often this involved having to take them into the garden and hose them down before they could go into the washing machine. When my turn came, I just tried to keep a smile on my face (well-practised with the kids) and think about the relaxing gin and tonic I'd be drinking later and pretend it was nothing at all to be wiping diarrhoea out of your mum's hair and picking it out of her fingernails.

The practical aspects of care took us all on a steep learning curve. It took us a year to work out that she needed regular chiropodist appointments, that we could get someone to come to the house and do her hair, that grooming was a constant, repetitive job to keep her looking halfway like the woman she had been.

It was an emotional learning curve too.

Mum could be difficult and defiant and angry and unreasonable. At least she had an excuse. I behaved like that just because. There were times I literally had to leave the room and walk into the other lounge and scream into a cushion. Then, I would rearrange my face and return, a smile fixed on my lips to distract from the tears in my eyes.

It wasn't just the dramatic stuff that tipped me. Often it was the totally mind-numbingly mundane. My mum was now a silent shadow of herself, able to talk but not make much sense. Not be the 'talker' she had been. On my weekend visits, I would spend the guts of two and a half days in a room with her and the TV. One-sided conversation becomes a strain. Weekend after weekend after weekend, trying to entertain Ruby and sometimes the girls, while just sitting with my mum was increasingly challenging.

I remember once as a difficult teenager, when I was going through a particularly trying time, my mum had sat me on the bed and said, 'Alana, I love you, but I don't like you very much right now.' It hurt. And it stayed with me, and while I knew I was loved, I also wanted to be liked. As a parent now, I see how strong that was. How important it was for her to differentiate between her unconditional love for me and her intolerance of certain behaviour. The boundaries she set for me all formed part of the wall of love she built around me. So here I was, slam-dunked into the Sandwich Years. I loved her unconditionally, but I didn't like who she had become.

But she had stuck by me through good and bad times, she had loved me even when she didn't like what I was doing, she had given me her time even when I had had no time for her, when I gave her sleepless nights and worry-wrecked days. That was her job. And this was now mine, whether I liked it or not. Just like she did anything for me, and I would do anything for my girls, I would now do anything for her too. Because love is a chain, and we are all linked together.

But another intricacy of this chain is that caring for a parent is not a singular job. Often there are two parents to care for, and while Mum's care occupied most of our time and attention, I couldn't forget about Dad and the emotional support he needed. Dad had become a full-time carer overnight, and while I found it hard enough to look after Mum at weekends, he did it day in and day out. And it wasn't easy. She was often scared and confused, difficult and upset. So often for the children, there are two caring roles going on simultaneously. For my brother and me, it was caring for Mum's physical health while keeping an eye on Dad's mental health. While I lay in bed at night with a monitor connected to my baby's room, listening out for little coughs and jumping out of bed when she needed me, so Dad now lay in bed every night with a monitor connected to his wife's room, listening out for little coughs that might mean vomiting, and jumping out of bed when she needed him.

I spent many a night sleeping in the chair at home with a baby or child in my arms. He spent many a night sleeping in the chair beside Mum in case she was sick. My brother and I had to factor in staying with my mum to enable Dad to get away on holiday and to get to see us in our own homes so he could have a break. Every so often, just checking in with him to make sure he was still coping. Making sure he looked after his own health needs.

The focus of our family was now caring for Mum. But actually it became about caring as a family for each other. My brother flew in from Edinburgh as often as he could, often working on his laptop beside Mum. (A bit like Chandler from *Friends,* I've never quite worked out what he does — something to do with computer software, so luckily he could sometimes work remotely.)

He was juggling the needs of his family, his job and our parents. It affected the whole family. My sister-in-law, Charlotte, sometimes came and cared for my mum to give Dad a rest and the impact on their family life was significant.

My husband looked after our girls on his own many weekends so I could be with Mum, and occasionally took time off work so I could get up to Belfast during the week. My family is close, muddled, imperfect, tempestuous, frightening, comforting, great and awful. I feel at home there. Every family is a hotchpotch of turmoil and contradiction, and our family has had more than its fair share of aggravation and dysfunction. There is not a family that does not wrestle with mental health issues, money issues, and interpersonal conflicts. Our issue led to years of strife where stress was rife and tensions rippled, but amid all the familiar family frustrations, there was always a quiet, strong love.

The Sandwich Years turned history on its head and the love shone through. We worked as a team. When I was upset, I cleaned or painted Mum's nails. When my brother was upset, he Googled and came up with a new practical plan. When my dad was upset, he made something.

There was one particular phone call I never expected to receive. My brother was over visiting my mum and he had decided to wheel her around to a friend's house nearby for a change of scenery. I begged him to dress her in something decent, brush her hair and put on a bit of lipstick. My mum had always been so glamorous, so well turned out. As she grew older, it took her longer and longer to get ready in the mornings. She would moan about how her hair and eyelashes were thinning. (Really, life? On top of everything else, you have to thin out our eyelashes!)

Sometimes I would sit on the bed and watch her 'put her face on', and she would stop trying to comb her hair into shape and turn to me and say, 'Perhaps I should just let myself go.'

We would look at each other, and then smile.

'No,' she would say, and turn back to the mirror to roll some mascara into her ever-diminishing lashes.

Now, it was horrific to see her lie as an old, old woman with grey lacklustre hair and no colour in her cheeks. Whenever I went to see her, I would put on her jewellery and some makeup and she almost looked like her old self.

My brother and dad were so great with my mum but, to be brutally honest, they're men. My dad, having completed the wheelchair ramps and drying hoists to keep up with the demand for sheets and nightwear, persisted to cook meals — that mostly went uneaten — make jam and her favourite date squares. He even made me my Christmas cake. He had many, many, many skills. Makeup was not one of them. I had tried to explain colour coordination to both Simon and Dad but they had simply stared at me, uncomprehending. These are two very intelligent, scientifically trained brains of bursting knowledge that usually left me confounded, but the concept of not putting navy and black together flummoxed them. Mum did have a tendency to look like the Wild Woman of the West in their care, but that was OK.

So on that summer morning, as I was at home hanging out the washing, an hour after we had first spoken about his idea, my brother called back. He needed guidance. He had made sure Mum had some good clothes on and some pretty jewellery. But he now stood opposite her, staring into the mystical abyss that was a woman's makeup bag and he needed me to tell him what to do. So I found myself standing in my kitchen with a cup of tea, phone in hand, directing my forty-six-year-old brother on the intricacies of powder blush and lipstick and how to apply foundation to his mother.

'Is it meant to leave a brown ring around her face?' he enquired dubiously.

I'm not sure how she looked in the end, but he tried. And I love him even more for it. Becoming a carer, in whatever capacity that takes, is a steep learning curve that takes trial and error. And that was what a huge part of life during those Sandwich Years was all about. Learning and adapting.

5

Limbo Grief

Grief is more than an emotion. It becomes a physical part of you, like shrapnel embedded in your flesh, as real and permanent as your arm or leg. It is always there. Although you might seem to heal and live with the scars, it is hidden in your bones, a pulse in your brain, a ticking in your heart. The hardest part about my Sandwich Years, or reaching this stage of life, is that you are often caring for someone you love while coping with this extreme grief.

You are often grieving while the person you are grieving for is still alive.

You are grieving for someone who is no longer the person you are grieving for. It is so hard.

For me, it was like the grief of my miscarriages, very private and with no funeral to show an open display of finality. I call it limbo grief. Grief for a death you cannot hold, but one that walks beside you all the same.

The days after my mum's stroke, the grief

felt like a physical assault. I was constantly under attack and I lived in permanent terror that she would die. The only real grief I had experienced in my life before this were my miscarriages, a limbo grief that is hard to define. Ironically at the time of those losses, I used to think that if my mum died, people would know what to do or say. It would be such an obvious grief. There would be a funeral and I would have a proper goodbye. Miscarriage is so private. Most people don't know it's happened, and those who do have no clue what to say. Those babies weren't real to anyone else but me.

The spring I was pregnant with what would be my first miscarriage, as I played with Daisy and Poppy in the garden, I noticed there weren't any butterflies. The girls were exploring their new world with wonder and I was eager to show them how wonderful it could be. But no butterflies could be seen. When I came back from the hospital, knowing my baby had no heartbeat, and sat in that same spring garden, I was at a loss about how to deal with my loss. How do you grieve for someone you can't bury but who you love all the same? And suddenly a butterfly flew past me and landed on a nearby rose. Its simplicity and beauty made me smile. I knew then what to do. Like that butterfly my little baby had not been destined for a long life. Its time was measured in weeks. And like a butterfly it had caught my breath as it danced and dipped into my dreams, fluttering and fragile, just out of my grasp. I bought a little silver butterfly for my charm bracelet and attached it beside the gold and silver heart I had for Daisy, and the silver star for Poppy. And just as our house jingled to the jangles of their laughter, our garden swayed with the colour of daisies and poppies and a little butterfly now danced along with them, there and on my bracelet.

Little did I know then that I would add another three butterflies to that bracelet. And that my bracelet would soon carry another significant charm.

★   ★   ★

On the day after that awful night when everything changed for my family, I had come home to my girls from the hospital and had been shocked by their joy. In such a short space of time, grief had robbed me of its memory.

I had held Ruby tight and smelled the top of her newborn head and tried to regain that bubble of pure love and joy that had been so brutally burst. Even the sweet sickly smell of her rancid nappy was a suck-it-in-it's-gorgeous moment. I had held my girls and listened to them prattle on. Two miles up the road, I had sat surrounded by death and disintegration, but here, at home, with the sun streaming through the kitchen window, they had reminded me again of life.

I remember standing up, distracted by a thought. All evening I'd known there was something I needed to do but I hadn't been able to put my finger on it. It was some routine I had forgotten and it had pestered me until I'd walked past the phone and automatically picked it up. I had gone to dial. And then I'd realised what the thing was. I hadn't rung my mum.

Slowly, I'd put the phone down, her number left undialled.

I had lain open-eyed in the dark that night, waiting for Ruby to wake for her feed so I didn't have to be alone.

When a situation is too overwhelming, we often compartmentalise or reduce it to smaller, manageable pieces. I hadn't even been able to contemplate my mum dying. Hadn't even been able to grasp a smidgen of thought about the enormity of that. I had never breathed in a world where her breaths weren't somewhere in the air, so I had focused on the smaller piece. And the loss I kept coming back to was for her hands.

My mum had had a hands-on approach to love. There were hugs and cuddles and bedtime snuggles. Touches and tickles and bedtime kisses. Her tongue could lash me too, but I'm glad of it. It gave me my moral compass and it all combined to make me who I am today.

She would always take my hand or throw her legs over mine on the sofa, always be the one to tell me to sit down and have a cup of tea. But it is her hands that fill my childhood memories — our hands embedded in a bowl of cake mix, our hands entwined on the sofa, her hands knitting me jumpers that were always too long but which I still can't throw out, her hand stroking my face goodnight. They stroked my hair when we watched TV, they stroked my back when I couldn't sleep.

As Mum clung to life in those first few hours, I had clung to her hands. I held them tight and the desperation of thinking I might never hold them again nearly broke me. I thought she was dying and that her hands would never touch me again. Her hands were the symbol of her love for me. They represented the catch element of my life so I was free to fall. They were the anchor that moored me. They were the stroke of calm, so I could strike out and be wild. And as I realised that I was being slowly cast adrift, it was her hands I needed to hold on to most.

It had come to me in a frantic moment, that night while I was feeding Ruby in the dark of my bedroom, what I was going to do. The following morning I had grabbed the print ink kit I'd bought to take Ruby's handprint to make cufflinks as a present for my husband. The company sends you out a special kit, and you are able to make the prints into mini pieces of jewellery. I took it instead into the hospital.

When no-one was looking, I pulled the curtain around Mum's bed. I don't know why I wanted to hide it — maybe I was afraid someone would think I was trying to get her fingerprint to embezzle hidden fortunes! I pressed her hand into the ink, gently pushing each finger into the softness, and then set it down firmly on the special paper card. Mum was still sleeping most of the time and her eyes remained closed while I did this. She barely acknowledged what I was doing. She had a black inky hand for days afterwards, but thankfully no-one ever asked why.

I sent off the handprint, and it came back as a silver heart charm with her handprint in the middle. It is attached now to my bracelet which has a charm to represent some of the things I love in my life. There is one for each of my girls, a butterfly for each of my babies that didn't make it, a starfish to represent my love of travel, an opened clam to remind me the world is my oyster if I work for it and, from that moment, a handprint of my mum, her hand forever holding mine, forever guiding me across the road. A daily reminder of the real hidden treasure in my life that I didn't need to embezzle: her handprint of love on me.

Every day, I mourned the loss of all that could have been, as much as what was.

People say time is a healer, but it is also the blunt knife that cuts deeper. Sure, time softens the pain and the heart-stopping terror, leaving behind a low-level ache. But the knife of time cuts deeper than that, reminding us over and over again that as life is moving on, we are leaving someone behind.

Long before Gwyneth Paltrow stepped onto the Tube in *Sliding Doors*, I knew what it was to live parallel lives. As a child, at unhappy or uncertain times, I would shift my head into another world while my body carried on with real life. But now as the Sandwich Years took hold, I found myself living parallel lives every day. Not for some wild escapism or some far-flung adventure, but simply to soften the blow of what was. My life had changed forever, for the worse, so, in my grief, I clung desperately to what should have been.

In this limbo grief, I was trying to come to terms with losing the mother I knew and adored, while learning to deal with the reality of a mum who barely knew my name and certainly couldn't say it.

We would never again share intimate chats about nothing and everything. We would never hold hands walking down the street. She would never walk into my house and say, 'Oh, isn't it gorgeous! Have you rearranged those cushions differently?' Nobody else ever noticed these things.

From the night my husband walked into my hospital room, my life split in two — the life I had planned, and the life I was forced by circumstances to now live. As I adjusted to this new world, in my head I lived through daily phone calls and regular visits where Mum would hold my baby in her arms, adoring her with songs and praise, while making me sit down for a cup of tea. I lived the experiences I knew we would have had, enjoying endless cups of Earl Grey tea together, with 'a little bit of something nice', reading stories to the girls, showing Ruby off to every person in every queue. My mum was the Martini Girl of chat — she could talk to anybody, anywhere, anytime.

Now I stood alone in my kitchen, phone in my hand but no number to dial. I would stand, bereft in the moment, and close my eyes. I would picture her coming off the Belfast train, a hundred memories merged into one real moment. I would be at the gate of Connolly Station, searching the crowd streaming from the train for her familiar ash-blonde hair, combed and prodded into shape, her familiar dark blue jacket, her eyes, cornflower blue, lighting up as she saw me, her wave. The smell of Estée Lauder's *Beautiful* greeting me with her warm hug, and then she'd be off. 'I met such a lovely woman on the train,' and breath would barely be taken as she told me tales of her conversations with the woman on the seat beside her or the man opposite, all the way home.

And as she walked through my front door she would say, 'I love coming to this house,' and we would sit down with a cup of tea, children scurrying around us, and she would be proclaiming Ruby to be the most beautiful baby she had ever seen. I lived every imagined memory of the future that didn't happen, to get me through the present.

But grief is like walking through a hail of knives and you never know when you are going to be cut by it. Especially when all those 'firsts' start flooding in.

★ ★ ★

For me, it was that first Christmas just three months after her stroke. As a child, I had always helped Mum to decorate the tree, and as I had grown and had Christmas trees of my own, Mum bought me little decorations, so that my collection grew up as a mixture of my past and my present. For us, Christmas really begins when the first red poinsettias arrive in the shops. Mum always bought one, and as soon as I had a place of my own, I began to as well. That year, wandering through the shops, every sighting of a poinsettia was a stab of pain. But I forced myself to buy not just one, but two. One for her and one for me. I would have to buy them for her now.

I went to Belfast and decorated her tree while she sat in her wheelchair watching, but mostly sleeping. I put on her favourite Christmas CD from King's College Choir, but she made no response to it. Dad set up the tree, and brought down the old battered box from the attic full of the same decorations we had hung when I was a child, many of which were so old they had come from her own childhood house. In the past, as we had hung our history on the tree, she would have a story for them all, but this year it was me who had to tell her the stories. She wasn't really interested and I could barely speak with the choke of loss in my throat.

And then there, at the bottom of the battered box, was the little white church that had belonged to her father, Jimmy. It was nothing special, not an antique, just a plastic white church with peeling gold paint that played a festive tune, but it always had centre stage in my parents' house because it reminded Mum of her childhood Christmases. I took it out, plugged it in and wound the little key. It lit up and for the first time since we started decorating the tree, so did her face. The figurine played its music and Mum belonged somewhere again.

But Christmas itself still loomed. Mum and Dad had been due to come down to us and, like every year, I had planned to take her and the girls to the National Concert Hall to hear the orchestra play *The Snowman* live to the film on the screen.

On Christmas Eve, we would all sit down to the Christmas ham dinner and then wrap ourselves around the fire, wine glasses glistening in the light of the flames, stuffing Santa sacks.

In the morning, as the girls, giddy with

Santa surprises, shouted 'Nanna, look!' when her sleep-bedraggled head curled around our bedroom door, she would sit on our bed and share their excitement. We would all have a walk in the crisp winter weather and then Mum and I, a little drunk perhaps, would try to produce a Christmas dinner in the right order before finding just enough room for a couple of chocolates by the fire at the end of the night.

Instead, that first Christmas, their car did not arrive, bringing bags and bottles of goodies. I didn't book any tickets for the National Concert Hall. I hung up the lights and carefully placed decorations around the house, knowing they would never be seen by the person who would appreciate them the most. And when it hurt too much, I slid open the sliding door and for a moment allowed myself to live the version in which their car drove up and they bundled into the house laden with love and presents. And I still heard my mum say, 'Oh doesn't the house look beautiful!' just because she had said it so many times before.

Instead, that year, my brother's family and mine all descended on my parents' not-big-enough house in Belfast, people and grief strewn everywhere. On Christmas Day, as my mum lay paralysed in her permanent bed and we pretended to be merry, the sliding door jammed and I could no longer soften the blow. This was how it was now.

Unable to swallow the food, I ran from the table and sat in the other room and howled. But I still had to make this the happiest day for the girls, so I got up, gathered my face and returned to the room, where we laughed and squealed with delight and tried to bring Christmas to this awful, awful farce.

This was only the beginning. I would have to organise Ruby's naming ceremony knowing my mum wouldn't be there. Plan a family holiday without her. Walk past the phone and not pick it up. But every so often, there were moments. Moments when the sliding doors pulled back together. Moments when I would climb onto the bed beside her, the smell of my own Estée Lauder *Beautiful* rubbing onto her skin, and hold her hand. Occasionally the past and present were still in tune, but mostly they were divided by a chasm of grief.

★ ★ ★

Seven months after Mum's stroke, we went on our extended family week to the west coast of Ireland over the Easter holidays in April. The family week we'd had every year with my mum and dad, my brother and his family, and me and mine. The family week Mum and Dad had organised the previous summer. The family week that no longer involved my family. Not as it had been anyway.

The year before, I had been there with my mum. We had pottered on Wild West beaches, collecting shells with the girls, enjoying chocolate buns with our tea, sitting side by side with our faces turned to the sun or our shins roasting by the fire. This year, her absence was present everywhere. I had never imagined it was possible to feel so much pain without bleeding. And the pain continued, as the realisation dawned that the trauma would not end. The trauma was constant. This wasn't an emergency or an event. This was life. As my three girls delighted in the company of their cousins, the house was filled with their laughter, the laugher that had made my mum's life so happy. But she wasn't there to hear it. And amidst the noise of childish chatter, I would be suddenly struck down, paralysed on the spot, cup in hand, children scampering around me, lost in my loss. While the world went on around me, I was still. And in my stillness, I could see her; her blue fleece walking along the beach, her white T-shirt covering arms that were wrapped around Ruby to soothe her screaming teeth, her sun hat tilted back as the sun scorched her skin and the view scorched our eyes with its beauty.

A bloodless coup had taken place, with not a mark on my body but my head and my heart had been left beaten and bruised.

That bright spring week was one of the hardest weeks of my life, made more intense by the beauty of the landscape and the glorious weather, both of which my mum had always appreciated. So I tried to see it for her. I tried to feel it for her. I picked up shells for her and doing this gave me the strength to carry on, to enjoy the moments of pleasure with my girls as we pottered on those Wild West beaches, ate chocolate buns with our tea, and sat with our faces to the sun. And I tried to feel her with me still.

In the aftermath of the aftershocks, there are lots of potholes left to negotiate. My mum's birthday in May was one of these dips in the road. She lay at home in Belfast, locked in her body and mind, and for the first time in probably fifteen years I didn't spend the day with her. After Daisy and Poppy had been born, she would come down to Dublin and I'd take her out for lunch. We would while away a couple of hours nattering about nothing and everything, sharing each other's lunch, and always finishing up with 'a little bit of something nice' with our cuppa. Then we would come back to my place and I'd throw a birthday tea party for her with the girls. They would have helped make buns and they'd sing 'Happy Birthday' until they were hoarse. Then Mum would help me with Poppy's birthday party two days later, blowing up balloons, making top hats, a very sophisticated party treat involving a drop of chocolate in the bottom of a mini bun case, with a marshmallow on top, then another smaller dollop of chocolate and a Smartie. I'd had them for all of my birthday parties, and so now do the girls. Mum would be clearing up exuberant princess spills and smiling at the mess a bunch of toddlers can make. But Mum couldn't come down to me anymore, and because it was midweek and Daisy was in school, I couldn't get up to Belfast.

That year Poppy turned four, and her Princess Party was her first one ever without her nanna.

Every 'first' event without Mum cut like the first cut — her stroke. A body blow, painful and bruising. The memory of the previous year so sharp, it cut constantly into the wound opening afresh.

But the most challenging by far was the big family event where my mum would have made the word Family with a capital F. Ruby needed to be officially named. My husband and I had had a civil wedding in the Unitarian Church, and both my other girls had their naming ceremonies there too. In the aftermath of Mum's stroke, I kept putting off Ruby's ceremony but eventually it had to be done. Planning such an important event knowing my mum wouldn't be there felt almost like a betrayal. Knowing she would be put in a care home excluded from our activities so that my dad and brother could come felt akin to tarring her and covering her in feathers. Knowing there would be photographs that she would be missing from seemed like slapping her in the face.

When my dad and brother arrived, Poppy asked, 'Is Nanna coming?'

'No,' I had to say. 'She's not.'

So that summer, nearly a year after her stroke, we went ahead without her. Another dreaded milestone in the loss of my mum, a loss that happened while she was still alive. I still found it hard to comprehend how life could change so drastically on the tick of a clock. One second her life was intact, bursting with fresh promise as she held her new granddaughter, and the next second, irrevocably, drastically, calamitously shattered.

And my own life lay broken amongst those

pieces. It took just one second to change my life — from one shared with my mum, to many events, celebrations and days lived without her.

As with so many days during the Sandwich Years, there were two breads to be buttered: Mum wasn't there, but this was Ruby's day and she deserved for it to be amazing. In many ways, it *was* wonderful. We had a beautiful ceremony and I read out a poem I had written for her about the wonder of her life ahead. She was given a small globe and was told the world is hers to protect and explore and be part of. Afterwards, we threw a party in the house that spilled into the sun-brightened garden. My dad and brother kept me warmed by the family blanket of love and support my mum had worked so hard to create. My friends shared my joy, loyal and loving as always. And of course, so did my husband, Daisy and Poppy. All there for Ruby — our much-fought-for, much-loved child, so utterly beautiful, so beguiling, so wondrous.

But it wasn't the same. It could never be the same without Mum.

It was like suddenly eating toast without butter. Like discovering the red wine bottle is in fact empty, when you've just lit the fire after a very long day and gone to pour a glass. Loss was ever-present like an unwelcome guest, and he had brought his friend Guilt, who smelled and made rude jokes and threatened to ruin the party. Mum wasn't there, but something worse was. She was alive and in a care home while the family she had built and fought for and kept together celebrated being a family. The worst torture I could ever have conjured up for my mum was for her to be excluded from the family she loved. But it was done. She wouldn't be in the photos, glowing from the love of Ruby, and she wouldn't be in the video, beaming in delight.

But as I look back now, I realise she *was* there. In our thoughts, in our unity and in our conversation. Because she was the rock I stood on. And in the photographs I am glowing because she loved me. And in the video I am beaming because her love kept me going still. I was her daughter, and always would be.

★   ★   ★

We are all orphans-in-waiting. From the moment we are born, we are destined to lose our parents. The question is when and how.

Losing a parent — whether we are close to them or not, have had a great relationship with them or not, will miss them or not — is a catastrophic event in anyone's life.

I know several people who don't have the best relationship with one or even both of their parents, and the fear of losing them is still profound, not necessarily because of the loss of love but because of the loss of hope that a resolution will be found. Losing a parent is like being cast adrift. Learning to draw your own map is the hard part.

Losing a parent long before they die is a nightmare none of us is prepared for and, as I was to find out, 'letting go' is the only way to survive. The problem is, there is no Disney soundtrack with Elsa singing in the background. How do you grieve for someone who is still alive and whose eyes still light up when you walk in the room?

My mum was still alive, but the mum I knew had died. This limbo grief is a horror many people live through every day, one that rarely gets talked about. That most peculiar, most painful of states in which you lose your parent long before they die. But it is scarily common. With my mum it was a stroke. For others it is Alzheimer's or Parkinson's or dementia. In many of these degenerative diseases, the person you have loved all your life is constantly slipping away, and although you hold on tightly to their hand, they fly away like a kite in the sky. You have a grip on them, but they are flying too far away for you to ever grasp the real them again. You are caring and grieving at the same time. It is a hugely traumatic experience and, for me, the grief was excruciating.

The torment of wishing for my mum, every time I saw her, was tearing me apart. My C-section wound had long healed, but I still felt physically sliced open. The visceral needs of my children and my parents collided and were in danger of spinning me out of control.

Inside, I had an emotional drain that was bleeding out. I had spent months in shock and grief, reeling and railing against what had happened. I kept expecting to wake up and for it all to be over. At least with babies you know the phases that are trying are just that. Phases. Though with Daisy I had just tumbled from one shocking state (three-hour feeding) to another (potty training) in an endless cycle of dishevelled delusion, believing I'd figure it all out tomorrow whilst glowing in the glory of love and the smell of new skin. I imagined that George was also lurking somewhere doing DIY and 'The Wheels on the Bus' was filtering giddily in the background. Tomorrow never came but at least by the time I got to Ruby, I knew the feeds would get longer, and there would eventually, at some point in my future, be a day without nappies. (Burn the nappy bin!) The horror of Mum's stroke was that slow (almost-afraid-to-turn-around-and-face-the-truth-standing-behind-you-with-a-knife) realisation that this was not a phase. This was now life.

The idea of five stages of grief was proposed by Elisabeth Kübler-Ross in her 1969 book *On Death and Dying*. Unfortunately, there is no book that I know of entitled *On Death and Living*. I certainly had been through most of the stages: shock and denial. Tick. Anger. Tick. Bargaining ('if you please come back I'll stack the dishwasher properly'). Tick. Loss. Tick. Finally, hopefully, there is acceptance. Acceptance isn't always reached, but it's considered the 'end' of grief. I'm not a psychologist, and I'm only an expert in my own life — and even then I haven't really felt I've known what I was doing since about 1986 — but I personally don't think you ever get over a profound loss, you just learn to live with the scar. For me, acceptance itself is not just the end of grief, it is the hardest, cruellest, most horrific part of grief. It feels like a betrayal and it is especially hard when the person you are grieving for is still alive. In the early stages, you are holding on to what was, grieving what has been lost. You take comfort in the sliding doors of retreat to the place that is safe and full of shared Earl Grey tea.

The hardest part is letting go of all of that, the dream of what your life could or should be, and accepting what is.

So the letting go I had to do was a source of private grief too. There was no ceremony for friends and family. No eulogy. No outpouring of shared grief. But I had to let go because my children needed a mum who could function and my mum needed a daughter who could care for her. So I needed to let go of Plan A and start to get to grips with Plan B.

I still wasn't sure *how* to grieve though. I had a moment of her love, her handprint on my bracelet. But that wasn't grieving. Many people experience the loss of their parents, but just because it happens to almost everyone doesn't make it any less brutal. I would look around me and wonder why the streets weren't littered with the bodies of people dying with grief. That's what it felt like. A death inside myself, a withering, a shrivelling.

I've watched so many movies with that 'grief montage', where they play slow break-up music in the background, and it's all about lying around unwashed under the duvet eating pizza, the place scattered with beer cans, watching lots of telly. But I had two kids and a baby, a mother and father. I have a no-telly-during-the-day house rule. And I don't drink beer. My mum was alive and needed care and stimulation, my dad was amazing but needed support, my kids needed something on their plates to push around and not eat or, in Ruby's case, drop on the floor. I had to think about going back to work and you need to get dressed for that. Where was the movie that portrayed that?

People talk about the dull pain of grief but, to me, it is acute. It's sharp and slicing with a serrated edge. It jabs and pokes and cuts and pierces. You bleed and bleed so much you expect to see a trail of red following you down the hall. You can't stem the flow alone, yet only you can feel the pain. Only you can stand and take it. And take it you must.

I knew I had to let Mum go and so I had to open up the floodgates and let in that pain. I had to stand in the hail of knives and be lacerated by the cuts. There is a huge selfishness that is inherent in a mother-daughter relationship — most of us take for granted that they will care for us. I didn't want to let go of my mother as it would mean letting go of the person who had championed me the most. Our relationship was complex, and during all those visits up to my childhood home, I had to walk through the flashbacks of my teenage years. Through the bad memories — Mum's overreliance on me, our fights over my striving independence — as well as the good — that sofa we had sat on to watch Mr Darcy jump into the lake (we had watched the BBC *Pride and Prejudice* box set so many times), and that mixing bowl in the kitchen in which our hands had worked together.

But selfishly, most of all, I missed her kindness. Her loyalty. Her dogged belief in me, belief that I was a good person. I was her specialised subject. She had shone a light on me. Sometimes that light was harsh like the lights in those changing rooms that highlight blemishes (ones I hoped were chocolate smears but were in fact age spots) and show up my imperfections. Sometimes the light had soft filters making me better than I really was, an airbrushed version of me. But mostly, it was a spotlight that made me feel stand-out and special, and I knew no-one would ever feel that way about me again. Who was going to call me a bitch when I was one, and still love me anyway? Losing that person, it's like taking off your armbands and just hoping you have the strength to keep paddling.

* * *

By that first summer I had fallen apart and picked myself up so many times I was dizzy. My two girls kept me motivated, my husband kept me alive. But when the doctors had told us my mum could live for years like this, I actually wanted to fall into the dark pit that was calling me. It was still a daily struggle. Grief is a unique experience for everyone and some will reach its stages sooner than others. For me, it was almost a year before I could begin to understand that something had to change. Mum wasn't going to, so that left just me. And it was in a place that was a part of my past, but also very much a part of my present, that I realised what I needed to do.

Donegal, on the far northwest tip of Ireland, is like one of those bad boys my mum had always warned me about. Moody and unreliable, glorious one moment, dumping you the next, but always irresistible. We used to go there when I was a child; just thinking of it, so many memories merge into one mishmash of nostalgia. Then, the potholed meandering roads made it a five- or six-hour journey from Belfast, and it was a major expedition. I can still close my eyes and see the rugged mountains and coastline, taste the chicken Maryland we had as a treat every holiday in the Nesbit Arms Hotel in Ardara, smell the turf, hear the silly names my brother and I gave all the funny-sounding Irish places. But mostly I remember my mum's white Tupperware box, always full of the fudge squares and caramel slices she had made the night before we left. The glorious days on the beaches, the long walks as my dad dragged us over 'just one more hill', the interminable days inside the smoky cottage as the rain lashed outside. Like every classic Irish holiday, there was the BBQ on the beach under an umbrella in the lashing rain, our teeth clenched in a 'we WILL have fun' sort of way.

Donegal has a personality complex. When the weather is clear, the horizon is further than anywhere I've ever been in the world. The sky seems endless, life limitless. But when the dark clouds brood and close in, spewing torrents of 'wet rain' like sheets of water, the sea mist creeps around until there is nothing in your vision at all — just you, your house and if you're lucky, the end of your path. No sky. No mountains. No road. Donegal can make you feel tall and small in one day. That smell of turf burning takes me back 30 years in an instant to my family sitting round the fire: life at its most basic, the rain thrashing the windows as the clump of the Tupperware lid opened and our family hands tangled in desperation, grasping hold of Mum's homemade treats.

And so that summer, I took the girls up there again. Same landscape, same smells, except I was the mum now. The schizophrenic weather had us changing clothes three times a day. I knew that if Mum hadn't had her stroke, she and Dad would have joined us for a few days, and we would have taken windswept walks along the cliffs, and collected shells on the beaches, and I know without a doubt that if she had been able to come, the Tupperware box full of homemade treats would have been on her knee as their car came up the drive.

But she never came. My month in Donegal, often alone with my thoughts at night, allowed me to contemplate, and remember, and start to allow myself the release of coming to terms with it for the first time. It was a Saturday morning. My husband had come up the night before for the weekend, and I slipped out of bed early, and quietly left the house. The girls would all be piling in beside him soon. It was one of those Donegal days, light emerging from the night like a halo of promise. As I walked the windy little road towards the beach, the hedgerows and trees sang to me, vibrating in the breeze and the flurry of activity from birds and insects. The very landscape was alive and bright and glorious and it made me feel a part of something magical. I jumped down the little dune onto the still, silent sand to find an undisturbed beach, glistening pools and curves in the sand the only sign of movement as the tide gently receded. As the dawn widened, so did the sky, bright, light, and glorious. I walked and I walked and I felt simultaneously bereft and lifted. Eventually I sat on a rock, and stared across the sea and out to the horizon. Without knowing how or when it started, I was shocked to discover I was sobbing. Sobbing for everything that I wanted but couldn't have. Everything in my life, even this moment, alone in one of the most beautiful places on earth, was tainted with my loss. And it was then I knew. I needed to be able to feel the joy again of sitting somewhere so glorious, and not be saddened. I couldn't live with this pain anymore. And I realised it wasn't the pain of loss that was constantly crushing me. It was the pain of holding on.

I walked back along that beach, crying, in pain, but also with a relief, knowing that over the next few weeks I had a difficult thing to do, but a necessary one. When I arrived back at our rental cottage I took a deep breath and went inside. A part of letting go was being able to remember the good times, take the treasures of our life together and our love and bring them into the future, but also accept the situation for what it was.

With a heavy heart, and a happy memory, I opened up Mum's recipe book which I had brought with me, and I began to make her fudge squares. That afternoon, after a wild swim in the sea, we all tumbled back into the house and lit the fire, and I brought out my tin and when it clipped open, our family hands tangled as we reached in for Mum's homemade treats. Once again, they became the holiday special. My girls now love them too, and so it continues. My mum would never share a holiday with us again, but as we sat in the turf-smoked room, the rain dancing furiously outside, I could remember the ones that we did share. Like Donegal weather, life is unpredictable. You never know what's around the corner. But like Donegal, it is the things that stay the same that keep life going. I missed my mum, but as I began to let her go, I started creating new memories in her shadow. Memories I hoped my girls would take through their lives as mine took me.

After a year of hating every second of being with Mum, hating the loss of what I was missing, I allowed myself to see the bits I still had. I returned home from Donegal with a new determination, knowing I had to do that terrible but necessary thing. On the next Friday afternoon, I drove up to spend the weekend with Mum and, as I hugged her and kissed her hello, I knew I was finally saying goodbye. I stroked her cheek and I held her hand and told her with my eyes that I loved her. I think hers told me to cover my cleavage. (My mum would always cover up my cleavage and now my daughters do it . . . my cleavage just wants to be free.) And then I took their big black dog, Jake, for a walk. I walked around the park that I had walked around with Mum for so many years of my childhood. I sat on the seat at the top and looked over at the Belfast Hills. I cried and I felt pain like I had never experienced before. And then I looked up to the sky and with tears flooding my face I whispered the words I needed to say to let my mum go. I said my goodbyes, and I told her I would always love her and have her. And when I was fit enough to stand, I walked back to the house and in through the door, and I looked at my mum and smiled, and picked up her hand. I would love her as ferociously as before, but in her own right. I would love her now for who she was, not for who I wanted her to be.

Then finally I had a weekend with my mum that was actually enjoyable again. I even smiled a real smile, and my shadow joined in. We hugged, we laughed, we connected. She even asked me a question, which was very rare. 'How did you sleep?' And I could honestly tell her I was beginning to sleep well again. We spent a wonderful day with her friends who still call themselves 'The Girls' despite being septuagenarians. We all hung out, laughed, drank wine and lifted our faces to the sun. My mum was upset afterwards, for she knew she couldn't talk to them properly, couldn't make herself understood, was muddled and mixed, and couldn't do anything to help, but I told her no-one minded. We all loved her regardless of how she was. She had certainly loved us for long enough. And on that drive home to Dublin, I didn't cry. Perhaps I even smiled with the glow of a weekend spent living. A weekend spent loving. Perhaps I should have checked my rear-view mirror to see if George Clooney was in the car behind.

6

Minding Your Head

As I grieved and cared in tandem after Mum's stroke, I often found it hard to be the adult when I wanted to be the child. The person I needed to call to make me feel better was no longer available. That's what I had always done when something good, funny or tragic happened: I had picked up the phone to Mum. But now she lay in suspended animation, a still frame in a world of moving pictures.

We were all moving on, but I had to try and take her back.

I showed her photo after photo from years of albums and told her the stories she had told me, her stories. But so many of them had been forgotten. First by me, because so many times growing up and, worse still, grown up, I had rolled my eyes and failed to listen. And now she had forgotten them.

Memories and moments in time, forever lost in her bleeding brain.

I know I'm lucky that I had a great relationship with my mum. It was fraught and fiery and complicated and caring and comfortable. I know many people who don't have that. I don't know if our grief is worsened or lessened by how our relationships are — by having something and losing it, or not having it and knowing you never would. But grief is grief. It's a big black hole you have to climb out of with a ladder made of supports — and for me that was friends, therapy, the occasional gin and help. But there is no easy fix.

And, sometimes, when grief and stress become overwhelming, we need help to break through them.

★   ★   ★

According to the World Health Organization, the number of women being diagnosed with depression has been on the rise, and is most common between the ages of forty and fifty-nine.[5] Is it a coincidence that this is the general age group of the Sandwich Generation?

Many of us have now been blessed with the ability to 'have it all', but sometimes it just feels like we 'do it all', and it can have a damaging effect on our mental well-being. A bustier-clad *Wonder Woman* was all over the TV when I was young, and now botoxed

Wonder Women are all over the media (or so it seems). But life is not a glossy magazine.

Some imperfections can't be injected or airbrushed out. Sometimes life is shit, and when the fan spreads it all over the walls, you can be overcome by the fumes. Sometimes you just have to ask for a gas mask.

When I was young, and my mum would say, 'I'm off to put my face on', she meant her makeup but she also meant it philosophically. She would put her face on to greet the day, no matter what was going on. Growing up, though, sometimes I saw that her facade slipped, the strains of her own life making the day impossible to face. She would be upset and clearly overwhelmed by her life at that time, juggling her relationships, childcare, parent-care, a job, a home. So while I learned from her how to always put my face on, I also knew how easily it could slip.

While I had come to terms with my mum's stroke, by the end of that first year my face was beginning to slip too, no matter how much makeup I applied. I had always known where I was going. Always had a plan and a list. But as childbirth hormones, grief and overwhelming stress built up, for the first time in my life, I felt completely lost. There was no guidebook sitting in the bookshop that could tell me how to deal with extraordinary and debilitating grief, how to nurture a baby, raise my children, how to rebuild some sort of career and look after a mother who needed twenty-four-hour care and a father who *was* that twenty-four-hour care. As the months went by, I had slowly morphed from dynamic to desperate to depressed. I was free-falling and I didn't know how to open my parachute.

Some people talk about depression as if it has a personality. A black beast or a dark demon. That makes me think of the Dementors in the *Harry Potter* books: fierce, faceless fumes of darkness. But my depression was different. It was more like a vacuum cleaner. It just sucked the life out of me and hoovered up all the crumbs.

In those first few months, the new routine of our new life took its steely hold. Daily phone calls to Dad, weekend drives up that motorway. At night I would lie in the dark listening to the clock tick, hoping against hope that Ruby, sleeping beside me, would awake so I didn't have to stare into the darkness alone; and yet, I was also hoping against hope that the morning wouldn't come.

I had no desire to pull back the curtains and search for a glimpse of the sky. There was no filtered music, no banners flitting between the clouds and I'd forgotten who George was.

Then Ruby would slowly stir beside me, that shuffle of sleepy muscles, the gentle squeak with the stretch of legs, a couple of shucks and sucks as her mouth found its tongue, little fists rubbing into little eyes before her brain found her voice and the day began.

My husband would sit up and reach for the light switch and I would sit up and reach for my smile switch. Because it was no longer a natural instinct to smile. I had to remember to do it.

As my husband would go down to get me a cup of tea before he headed off to work, two little heads would appear around the door and snuggle under the duvet while I lifted Ruby out of her carrycot and fed her.

With my cup of tea brought, I could look in the mirror opposite and behold a perfect scene, unbrushed hair and un-airbrushed face notwithstanding.

I would get up and the morning mayhem would begin, of getting the girls dressed and breakfasted for school.

Being a busy doctor, my husband left early so usually it was one big person pushing to move everyone forward, to get them out the door, and three little people doing everything they could think of to do nothing at all. Ruby had to be changed, fed and dressed. Daisy and Poppy needed to be dressed and their long hair took a whole section of the morning routine to do up. Breakfast had to be put out, force-fed (yes, I'm admitting it), wiped up. Then they all had to be ushered back upstairs for the toothbrush challenge, the hide-and-seek shoe show, and the coats, hats and scarves frenzy. At this point, Ruby would go red in the face, loudly fill a nappy and then smile sweetly at me. Coats off, her clothes off and a rapid, rancid nappy change. Then, it was coats back on and the double buggy manoeuvred out the door, and the scooter set to go. As every mother knows, this never happens with filtered music and George Clooney holding the door open while you take the shins off yourself getting the pram out. It was a daily, daunting deluge of high-pitched screams and tantrums. The kids got upset too. When I got them all safely delivered and I had walked back home with Ruby, I would take a deep breath and call Dad.

I tried to be upbeat, helping him with any financial and practical decisions and forms that had become an important part of caring for the life of someone who was barely living. I would try and speak to Mum, chirping about the girls and Ruby, hoping she wouldn't catch the catch in my voice. Only then could I face the rest of the day, playing with Ruby and feeding her, collecting the girls and trying to smile and show enthusiasm for arts and crafts. I would cook and I would clean and I would bathe and I would bake and I would hug and I would chase and I would stroke and I would read and I would choke and I would hide and I would kiss and I would tidy and I would sob. I would try to quell my panicking heart.

Then, at weekends, I would pack up my bag and pack up Ruby's things and get in the car and drive for two-and-a-half hours, the grey motorway matching the palette of my mood. And I would spend the weekend in such pain, seeing my mum in this fractured, haunted state, I felt like I should be checking myself for blood. And my girls would call and I would chirp on and hope they wouldn't catch the catch in my voice. And then I would pack up my bags and get in the car and drive for two-and-a-half hours home, the first hour clouded by the tears of leaving my mum, but knowing I was really crying because she had left me.

I dreaded it. Every few months, we would sit down with the calendar and my brother and I would decide who would cover what weekend at Mum and Dad's. I would just score out calendar weekends, score out time with my family, score out the life I wanted to live. The deep, dark weight pulled from the pit of my stomach as I scored out those weekends, knowing I hated every minute of this situation, but knowing I could do nothing about it. Supporting one family often meant leaving the other.

When I took the girls with me to Belfast, that was almost worse. Mum had little mental stimulation because she couldn't read or really follow the TV and so she loved being touched. She loved having her hair brushed or cream rubbed into her skin. I would be in the former dining room with Mum, who needed time spent on her, and three small children, none of whom were remotely self-sufficient, and who needed help to play, paint and poo. For forty-eight hours.

They played with the remote control of Mum's bed, raising it up, lowering it down, raising it, lowering it down, raising her head, and (their favourite) raising her feet, until she gave me that look. Her eyebrow raised, that said, 'OK, I've had enough. I'm not a toy.'

So that was five minutes done. Only 2,875 to go.

The intensity of all their needs — all to be served by me! — was, at times, torturous.

What I found extraordinary was that there was no end in sight. The Xs marked on the calendar could go on for years. My mum needed me. My dad needed me. My children needed me. They all needed help. But soon I realised that I needed my help too.

I was bereft.

I was rendered lifeless, the sheer energy to keep walking and talking amid the responsibility for this baby, my children and my mum had eaten me up from the inside out.

I have always been a glass half full, solutions-seeking sort of person. Give me a problem and I'll find a way through it. The day I knew I needed help for what would be diagnosed as post-natal depression, although I suspect it was more like post-traumatic depression, was when the blackness in my heart and the fog in my head clouded the glass so much that it wasn't that I suddenly saw it as half empty — I couldn't see the glass at all.

I couldn't find my way anymore, and I had no idea how to manage the next hour or the next moment, never mind my entire life.

Ruby was a wonder, and just the smell of her would lift me. Poppy was emerging as a gentle creative little personality and she made me smile so much with her contradictions of wilfulness and calmness. Daisy amazed me every day with her smart, bright determination to make the best of everything in life. But the clouds were always there.

A few months after Mum's stroke I had started to have panic attacks in the evenings. These were terrifying, physically suffocating. Perhaps they came at that time because, as soon as I got the girls to bed, I could finally switch off the smile and, in doing so, the tears the smile had forced away rushed through me like a tidal wave and I would find myself drowning on the kitchen floor, gasping for air, clutching desperately at my husband's shirt while he tried to help me get my breath.

I did have life rafts. I had amazing friends who came from all walks of my life, who were (and are) my wing-women.

One was Amanda. We met in the jungles of Borneo too (must have been something in the rain-drenched air) and we had been through some great adventures together and also some great challenges. We met in a jungle of adventure and travel, and now adventured through our jangles of domestic life together. Some mornings when I got back from taking the girls to school, Amanda would just show up at my front door. We didn't have to speak. She just took Ruby out of my arms and walked into the kitchen to put the kettle on. Sometimes, I collapsed there and then on the floor by the front door, and cried while she made the tea. Amanda, my family, my other friends, and my husband were all so supportive, but they couldn't fix me. I needed more than a life raft that would deflate as soon as they left. I was mortified to be failing and so I kept the worst from them. My mum had entered a world that left her with no memory of her life before, and no curiosity about the days ahead. And I had entered a world I couldn't bear to be in. But I was a coper! I was a doer! I had a game face. And yet, I couldn't hide it anymore. I wasn't coping, I wasn't doing and my game face had morphed into a gargoyle.

★　★　★

It was during the first year of my new reality when it happened. On this particular day I had been standing in my lounge with Ruby in my arms. I don't think she'd been screaming, I don't think it had been any particular thing. I had just been so weary, so tired, so drained, I'd wanted everything to black out. It wasn't that I'd had any desire to die — far from it — but it was just that I had found it unbearable to live in those moments. I had swayed gently Ruby in my arms, watching the traffic on the road.

I'd watched the traffic and then, in a truly horrible moment of sliding doors, I had watched myself walk to the front door, open it, walk down the driveway and step into that traffic.

There had been no clarity, just cloud. There had been no freedom, just fear. There had been no peace, just panic. There had been no solutions, just insurmountable problems. I had no will. Just weariness. And I wanted it all to end. I hadn't just wanted a pause button anymore. I'd wanted a stop button.

But something had tipped the scales in my favour.

Perhaps it had been all those hugs I'd got as a child. All that love I'd had around me. I honestly believe there was only a 51 per cent chance of me doing what I did next, and a 49 per cent chance of following myself onto the road. I think it was my mum's love and my children's love all scrunched up and dense that had weighted that 2 per cent extra.

Instead of walking out the front door, I had stepped back through the sliding doors and picked up the phone. I had made that phone call so many times in my head, but always with the fear that if someone realised I wasn't perfect, the world would end. If I wasn't perfect, someone would take my children away, or take me away. But this time I had waited through the rings until my community nurse answered. She had cared for me after Ruby was born, coming round to check on her and, perhaps, aware of the situation with my mum, had given me support. 'Can you come around?' I asked in a voice as small as Ruby's.

I could hear her flicking through her diary. I found a stronger voice.

'In the next ten minutes?'

She had stopped flicking. 'Alana, are you OK?'

And for the first time, I'd told the truth on this one.

'No.'

I dropped onto the sofa and looked fearfully around me. I was surprised to see the world hadn't caved in.

'I'll be straight there,' I heard her say. I was still distracted, waiting for the walls to crumble. They never did.

I had admitted I was unable to cope and the world had not fallen apart. It was just me that was crumbling, just me that was falling apart. And I needed help to build myself up again. I think I had still been holding the phone when the doorbell had rung.

She had been amazing. As I'd wept out my worries that someone would take my children away if they knew I couldn't cope, she'd just held my hand and smiled. 'No-one is taking your children away. But I think we should see your GP.'

We walked around to my GP that morning, simple as that, and he listened, and he said the words that turned me around.

'You're going to be all right.'

He said it so casually, yet so convincingly that I knew he was right.

He'd explained that I had post-natal depression, which was hardly surprising, and prescribed me a mild antidepressant. He advised me that at some point in the future, when I felt a bit clearer, counselling might be helpful.

It had taken a few weeks for the medication to take effect but, when it had, it was like a cloud lifting.

The cloud had also been blown away by the words I had whispered: 'I need help.' They hadn't changed my situation. They didn't take away my grief. They didn't make my mum's legs work and they didn't come with a cleaner. They didn't stock the freezer with containers of pre-made, nourishing food. I still had all the work and responsibility I had before. I still had to drive to Belfast and, more often than not, leave my older children behind, and try to smile at the face of the mum I had lost. I still had to raise three small children and think about going back to work. On the face of it, I had been managing.

But as I was to discover, it wasn't me that had been doing all that. It was my shadow. All of it. Every smile, every tinfoil crown, every meal, every shoelace tied and lock of hair plaited. All my shadow's doing. The real me never sat up and switched on the smile in the morning. The real me was always still upstairs, lying in the dark, refusing to pull back the curtains. Finally I asked for help and that help enabled me to get out from under my duvet to join my shadow and press play.

I am not advocating medication for everyone. It worked for me for the short time I needed it, but everyone is different, and everyone copes differently.

*　*　*

My depression carried on for another year, through the ups and downs to Belfast and the depths of caring for my mum, and the downs and downs of parenting. There's meant to be an 'up' in that last phrase but it was hard to find the 'up' those days. It seemed to be downhill all the way.

Depression is a bit like a cold sore. It was there all the time, in me, just beneath the surface. Much of the time it was dormant, under the surface, away from public view . . . but in my system. Then, a small itch bubbled up. A weird feeling that something was wrong, but nothing to show for it. It brooded and boiled and then erupted. It erupted so venomously, so virulently that, even though it was just a small part of me, it would take over completely, and I walked around as if it was covering my whole face.

And as with a cold sore, you just have to bide your time.

What I didn't know then — but which I absolutely know now and want to shout bare-breasted, breast-beating and waving from the rooftops — is this:

**IT'S OK FOR THINGS TO BE HARD! SOMETIMES LIFE IS HARD.
YOU JUST HAVE TO ACCEPT THAT AND KEEP LIVING IT.**

Life isn't perfect or great all the time. Life can be shit. You just have to get used to the smell.

The struggle to parent is hard enough. The struggle to parent with no parent and to parent your parent at the same time can be overwhelming. Everything was hard those days. Making the breakfast. Wiping Ruby's uneaten breakfast off the floor. Getting four of us dressed, fed and out the door every morning. Getting my tasks done while Ruby slept. Deciding what to make for lunch. Making lunch. Wiping Ruby's uneaten lunch off the floor. Endless car seat manoeuvres, endless times a day. Deciding what to make for tea. Making tea. Wiping Ruby's uneaten tea off the floor. The bedtime routine. And then, finding the energy to start some freelance work again in the evenings when the children were asleep, bed calling. Driving up the motorway. Making Mum's breakfast. Wiping Mum's uneaten breakfast off the bed. Cleaning Mum and Dad's house. Painting Mum's nails. Showing her photos. Making her tea. Wiping her uneaten tea off the bed. Driving down the motorway.

★ ★ ★

Daisy, always one to slap me in the face with her words (as I had done a million times to my mum), threw me another punch one day. It was morning and I was under the normal duress of getting everyone up, dressed, fed and in some reasonable state to leave the

145

house. I was giving out about something when she just walked off, saying, 'Blah, blah, blah.'

My face stung with the brutality of her swipe.

That's what my voice sounded like to them now — white background noise. Blah, blah, blah. I even bored myself.

Everyone talks about the joy of parenting. Everyone talks about the sense of achievement and the sheer pleasure of children. We hear less about the bone-crushing monotony. The nerve-wrecking lack of validation. *The guilt*. The hurt, the frustration, the feeling of failure, the despair, the constant questioning of your parenting skills, the emotional punches, the lack of time to be yourself.

And yet, we wake up the next day and try and start it all over again, trying to make it better, trying to make ourselves better, and there is the sheer uphill exhaustion of doing it all again, but better, and getting to the end of the day more times than not feeling you fared worse.

I knew I had three amazing children. I wanted them to be amazed by me. I wanted my voice to be something of a building block in their lives. I wanted them to see how to live by watching me. I didn't feel as if I was doing any of those things. I had a choice: be 'Blah,

blah blah' or be a voice I wanted them to hear.

★ ★ ★

That time was the toughest struggle of my life, just learning to survive. Just to get to the end of each day. But slowly, slowly, I began to recover as the clouds lifted and I regained some control of my life. I stopped taking the antidepressants and muddled through on my own to stop the clouds descending. I wrote my journal and a blog I had created to write about experiences and I tried to get as much sleep as I could. I was gaining strength. My internal GPS had found a faint signal for my mojo again.

It also helped that Ruby was now a year older (and a year bolder). It helped that the girls were that bit more independent. It helped that we had started to get Mum up in her wheelchair for a couple of hours each day via a hoist and it helped that on sunny, warm days we could even walk her round the park at the end of their road.

It helped that I wasn't dealing with stitches and wounds, and bursting breasts and haphazard hormones. It helped that although I still dreaded the scored-out calendar, I no longer dreaded my mum; she didn't scare me anymore. I looked forward to seeing her and telling her all the news. Some of the time it made her smile. She could speak fully now, although more often than not, her thoughts were confused and she didn't make much sense. She recognised people but wouldn't be able to think of their names. I no longer hid from my girls in the bathroom, at times I was able to put everything else aside and play with them. I no longer winced when Ruby cried and held her arms up to be held, again; I swooped her up and made her giggle.

Finally, after a time of darkness, I started to see the smallest speck, the glimmer of shimmer, a tiniest touch of light. I just had to find my way towards it.

★   ★   ★

Mental health has always been the poor relation of physical health. But without mental health there is no health. Just as our bodies get ill or injured, so, too, do our minds. Just like our bodies need to be loved and looked after, so do our heads. Having post-natal depression worried me. I recovered but it scared me. I knew I had to mind myself so that I could continue to mind others.

I discovered that half of all mental

disorders have their onset during the school-going years. This terrified me! What my girls will experience, and how they cope, will have a profound effect on the rest of their lives. Girls face more and more pressure to be perfect from an earlier and earlier age, and this is a worrying phenomenon. I realised I will play one of the most important roles in making sure my girls can cope, are given the mental, emotional and practical skills to deal with family life, school life, social life, friends, academia and social pressures. So, I reasoned, I'd better learn how to cope myself!

My girls were just in primary school, but already I was dealing daily with issues relating to the general jamboree of the schoolyard. I could only imagine the challenges of the years ahead. According to Headstrong, the Irish youth mental health charity, as many as seven children per average school class are experiencing psychological issues.

We start young and we just keep on heaping stress on ourselves.

The research from the World Health Organization shows that nearly twice as many women as men are affected by a depressive or anxiety disorder. One in three people experience depression or anxiety — the majority of whom are women. Now *that* is a proper depressing fact on depression. Being overworked, undervalued, whether carers, careerers, in poverty, working outside the home and then returning home to do most of the housework and childcare can all weigh down on women. Throw in hormones (PMT, pre-natal, post-natal, perimenopausal, menopausal to name but a few), loss, grief and a myriad of other factors that life throws at us, and it is not surprising that women need help sometimes. Unipolar depression, predicted to be the second leading cause of the global disability burden by 2020, is twice as common in women.

I remember, after that summer in Donegal I had one of those mummy-madness moments. Feeling put-upon, stressed, overworked and undervalued, I asked my girls what makes a happy household. I meant it as a rhetorical question that would lead to my smart reply along the lines of 'A happy mummy makes a happy household and helping, doing as you're told, not fighting (yada yada yada) would make me a happy mummy.' Instead, I was stopped in my tracks. My bright little button Poppy looked at me and said simply, as if it was the most obvious answer in the world, 'Love, Mummy. Love makes a happy household.'

I dropped my doldrums and hugged her hard. She was right, of course. Love is the answer. But sometimes it's not enough. You also need practical help. Sometimes, when life is shit, you need to put on your gas mask.

7

Identity Crisis

For me, one of the most challenging aspects of being caught up in the Sandwich Years, outside of the grief, shock, and relentless pull on my time, was the loss of a clear sense of who I was anymore. As far as I was concerned, I no longer had an identity, or at least not one I recognised. So many needs pulled at me, my life was no longer defined by striving for things I wanted but instead by surviving and responding to the multiple responsibilities I had. I had no space, and no place where I could reveal my true face, because so many people needed me.

It's very easy to lose yourself in labels. We seem to lurch from label to label (sadly for most of us, not the designer kind). For a woman, the labels can include daughter, student, wife, career woman, mother, carer. Since my Sandwich Years began, and in the five years of parenting before that, I had been stretched and pulled and pushed and prodded until I no longer looked or felt like myself. And no, this is not just called ageing.

For me, it was not external (although I was not fond of my Wild Woman of the West look sometimes). This was an internal mirror, and I no longer recognised the reflection. The glass was smeared with confusion and no amount of Windolene was going to clear it.

For thirty-five years my life had all been about me, and finding myself was an adventure. Then, quite quickly, I became a wife, a mother and a whole load of other labels, lots of things to lots of people, and finding myself was like trying to find a matching sock in a huge basket of laundry — either impossible or too much of a chore.

I had become someone else entirely and I just didn't know who. I felt like that game where you put different heads and legs on bodies and make all kinds of combinations. I no longer knew which body fitted my head (I wished it was Julia Roberts' in *Pretty Woman*), and my feet were so busy running in different directions that they were more like swan legs paddling furiously under the surface.

When I became a wife, I became an extension of my husband. When I became a mother, I became an extension of my girls. The career I'd once had no longer defined me. The lines of who I was became blurred and as I emerged from the haze of babies and then grief, I no longer had a clear-cut vision of myself. In juggling so many balls as a wife, a mother, a daughter and carer, I took my eye off the one that had my name on it. I was having an identity crisis.

Loss of identity is something many women experience when they have children, and amidst dirty dishes and piles of washing, it can be hard to find ourselves again. In her groundbreaking book, *The Feminine Mystique*, published in 1963, Betty Friedan wrote about 'A problem with no name' — the loss of identity many women feel as partners and mothers. On one hand we are being told we can be anything we want but, in reality, we end up being so many things to so many people, we can often lose track of who we really are. Being a mother is amazing and fulfilling, but it also naturally sucks away much of the energy previously devoted to yourself. Throw in other elements of care for parents, partners, colleagues and friends, and facilitating other lives becomes a way of life at the expense of our own. The silent suffocation of self, often stoked by lack of confidence, fear and pressure towards perfection, can lead to a slow fading away of our passions, and our selves.

Before I got married and had children, I had been a career girl in every sense of the word. I was top of my game, playing the game and naming the game. I had always had a very clear sense of who I was and where I was going. I followed my passions for writing and social issues and had forged a very successful career doing what I loved in the non-profit sector.

Then, becoming a mother was like finding a secret door in myself. I never knew it was there but, when I opened it, there was a world of wonder and worry that would come to feel like home. It was unexpected. It was marvellous. It was challenging. As someone who loved her own space, that total invasion of space a child brings took some time to adjust to. Children gave me the freedom to love and live in a way I hadn't imagined. They also restrained me in a way I hadn't thought possible. I had travelled the world but when I became a mum, I entered a land with no map, no language skills and barely a suitcase of clothes.

Nothing had prepared me for the upheaval of having a baby. I have always been a doer and have never been afraid of hard toil. Working twelve-hour days were food and drink to me; burning the candle at both ends was a way of life. I thrived on lists and deadlines, there was always a plan, a place to go, someone to see, something to do.

I got pregnant immediately after our wedding. (I had thought it may take a year of trying — it took a week.) Being pregnant gave me more lists to write, new things to learn, and a whole new set of plans to make. I still have a copy of that ill-fated birthplan I made for Daisy, as a reminder of how my preordered life was turned upside down the moment I became a mother.

Eventually I had settled into a routine and I happily produced colour-coded charts for the fridge door to keep me in line for feeding, sleeping and playing as I raised one then two girls under two. I had never in a million years imagined that I would give up my career when I had children. But suddenly, instead of looking forward to going back to that high-octane, busy job, I realised I didn't want to leave them every day.

My job, before I had children, was Director of Fundraising and Communications at a busy national children's charity and it had been a seven-days-a-week commitment at times. The career that had driven and defined me all those years just did not seem as important compared to my new mission. And so I made a decision that surprised me. I was aware of the long line of women who went before me and who fought to ensure I had choices. And this was now mine.

I had always been brought up to believe I could do what I wanted as long as I worked hard. I had taken great leaps of faith before, giving up work to travel, moving countries on a whim. I knew I wanted to be with my babies, and so I took another leap of faith and believed I would figure out my work life again sometime in the future.

Feminism, to me, is about choice and potential and being free and able to make the decisions that make us the happiest. As a feminist, I felt right about making the decision to give up my job when I had my first child. It was a huge financial adjustment, because I had a good salary, and it meant giving up holidays and other luxuries. I knew I would have to work again soon, but not the way I had been. I had no idea how, I just knew I had to create a new career that would enable me to do what I loved as well as be around my girls. I had cast myself adrift from the career I had known, and hoped I could anchor myself again to something new that would make it easier to be a parent.

While it was an easy decision to make, it was not always an easy decision to live. There were moments when I stood over the ironing board wondering where I had disappeared to. Somewhere between childbirth and child-rearing, the workaholic iron lady had become the work-worn ironing lady.

My mum would arrive down on the Belfast train, and the first thing she would do when she settled into the house was say, 'Now put the kettle on there and let's sit down. Look, I brought a little bit of something nice to eat with it.'

And then while I sat, she would take out the ironing board and chat as she ironed out my housework. She even ironed my pants. The last photo of my mum before her stroke was her in my kitchen ironing my husband's boxer shorts. That was the last time we ever had smooth underwear.

So I gave up my job and, admittedly, at times it felt like I gave up my life. My job had defined me and now I struggled. I lost my job title, my financial independence, and with it, for a while at least, I lost my identity. Or so it felt. I often had to remind myself that this *was* my choice. I loved the freedom, I loved the newness of this life, and most of all I loved being with my girls. But, much as I loved and took delight in them as they progressed and developed, I also found it hard. Sometimes unbelievably, overwhelmingly hard.

It was often relentless, thankless, frustrating, lonely, frightening and all-consuming. It would be years before I could go to the toilet alone. I had managed a team of twenty people for God's sake, surely babies couldn't be this hard? I'd made a hundred decisions a day, managed multimillion euro budgets, hired and fired, and developed complex, long-reaching business strategies. Now, there were days when I could hardly decide whether one child needed a coat or a blanket, water or juice, courgette or broccoli purée. Working for an international aid agency, I had travelled without fear to war-torn countries but now found negotiating a double buggy through Grafton Street a major challenge. I had backpacked round southeast Asia with little more than a T-shirt and two pairs of knickers but now I found packing a change bag to go out for the day virtually impossible. Of course, being at home also meant I took on the lioness' share of the housework (by osmosis, as I never actually agreed to it!), and the days seemed to roll into each other in an endless blur of washing, ironing, hoovering and cooking.

Here I was taking a road so well-travelled that it came with its own section of guidebooks in the bookshops. A road so well-travelled that I didn't need to sit an exam. A road so well-travelled that I thought I'd know what to do. Sure, I eventually learned how to breastfeed, breast-pump and burp the kids; sure, I eventually got the knack of making them eat broccoli purée (mixed with pear), of potty training and of bedtime routines.

But it was as if the more I learned about being a mother, the less I knew about myself.

I loved being their mum. I think I even became quite a good one. But I lost a bit of me along the way, dropped as I bent down to pick up endless dirty pants from the floor.

In those early years, after becoming a mum, I thought I should look like one. I could have chosen Brooklyn and Harper's mum of course. Instead I chose to look like my own. While I liked that Mum was always well turned out and sometimes glamorous, I forgot she was also forty years older than me. I refer to these now as the Boden Years. (Online shop, very nice, very middle class, middle England. Nothing wrong with it whatsoever, but I didn't even buy from the young and trendy section, choosing from the same section as my mum.)

I had left a high-powered career during which I wore matching underwear, and entered into a world in which I couldn't even get my boobs to match inside a nursing bra. (Breastfeeding does that — one is always bigger than the other.)

I didn't know how to fit into this new

world, so I borrowed the brightly coloured catalogue from Boden and made myself into one of the women inside it.

In fact, my mum and I would often go through the catalogue together, and at times even bought the same tops. (Really, we did.) In my defence, Mum was quite a trendy, well-turned-out woman. But you know you've gone down a wrong road when even your mother-in-law greets you with, 'Oh I bought that dress too!'

I worked so hard, yet because I wasn't seen to be 'going to work', it didn't quite feel like I was contributing much. In fact, it was clear my children didn't think so.

'Please stop jumping on my sofa,' I said to Daisy one day.

'It's not *your* sofa,' she said defiantly.

'Excuse me?' I said even more defiantly.

'Daddy is the one who works. It's *his* sofa.'

I can't remember how I replied but I can still remember the deep feeling of being punched in my gut. Failure came and put his arms around my shoulders and walked me into the kitchen where Doubt was waiting. My loss of a sense of identity was profound.

When I was through the immediate baby-survival period with Daisy and Poppy, I began to think about what I might do for work again. I knew I didn't want to go back to a full-time, office-based job. I didn't really have a clear plan, but I thought about what I was good at, what I enjoyed and where my experience lay.

My hybrid new career started in the playroom when Daisy was still a toddler and Poppy was a wobbler, and grew organically over the next few years. I had always wanted to be a writer but the only writing I had really done had been part of previous jobs. One particular day, I wanted to explore my thoughts about this new world of parenting but there was no platform to speak them from. So I wrote them down. I started with a blank page, and ended up with what looked like an article. I sent it off. It got rejected. I made more puréed food and hoovered up the cat hairs and decided to send it off somewhere else. It got rejected.

I pushed the prams around the square and all the while my internal voice was building. I wanted to talk about how wonderful parenting was, but also how hard. I sent it off again and, that night, I wrote another page. That ended up looking a lot like an article too.

Then something funny happened. I got a call from the third magazine and a friendly voice said she loved my article, could she publish it, and did I have any more? I started blogging about parenting and found a whole community of men and women just like me. And so I set up my desk amid the clutter and clatter of my children, and began my first cottage industry, crafting words and selling them.

As my creativity mingled with my children's, our energies bounced together, chatting and jumping like the jack-in-the-box in the corner. Prams, half-dressed dolls, tired jigsaws and gaudy ponies with synthetic hair littered their lair. Paper, laptops, chewed pens and gaudy highlighters littered mine. Their half was wild and exploded, chaos in chemistry — a fairy in the doll's house, Lego pieces in the pen drawer, playthings as scattered as their bouncing brains. My half was neater and calmer, and duller. Blue and black files stacked tall, books piled precariously high, mounds of paper trails leading to my biggest toy, the computer.

Their bookcase was a rainbow of colour, mine a monochrome of monotony While their mouse ran up the plastic yellow clock, my mouse worked against the ticking clock, and deadlines began to loom. I sat at the desk, thinking, straining, one hand writing, the other stroking a child's hair while another toddled at my feet. And, at night, as they murmured in their sleep upstairs, heads still racing, but bodies limp with exhaustion, I sat in the noise of their silence and worked.

Soon after writing an article about books, I was given the job of reviewing books on an RTÉ daytime television programme. It was a tiny job but the feeling when the taxi arrived to collect me and I sat first in Makeup, then plonked myself on a couch to talk about my favourite books was extraordinary.

Gradually, I built up a little business of both writing and consulting for the charity sector, but because I had so many other commitments, it took up all my free time. My working hours were the ones left over when everyone had taken what they needed. Every minute was allocated to at least three different functions and craziness ensued.

A year after Ruby was born, I began to get back to my previous work consulting and writing. There was a certain guilt in leaving my girls if I had to attend meetings, as the logistics of childcare, organising meals, school pick-ups, and general family needs now whirled around the demands of work. And I had to factor in time to go to Belfast. Every minute was allocated — from 6 a.m. when I got up to walk the dog before my husband went to work, to the moment I lay my heavy head on the pillow, assuming at last this was my moment — only to have Ruby cry out. Nope. That moment wasn't mine either. All my moments were theirs. My weekends were theirs or my mum's. Sometimes the pie chart of my life had so many sections, it looked like a spliced apple.

Most women I know are the pivotal person in the home, responsible not only for themselves and their work, but for the household chores and family responsibilities, everything from children's birthdays, to family presents, to washing, cooking, shopping and buying clothes for everyone. On the whole, women facilitate other people's lives as well as their own.

According to Mumsnet in a survey conducted in 2014, women still do twice as many household chores as men.[6] Feminism gave women the chance to do good work. To be creative. To have goals that did not focus merely on money or the needs of others, but on their own ambition and creativity drawing from their skills, experiences and achievements. The only problem was, and for many still is, that no-one came along and took away our other work. And I started to feel this.

Not only was I working again, freelancing as a writer and a fundraising consultant for charities, caring for a mum and dad and three children, I had also ended up cleaning two houses: my parents' and my own.

Before I got married, I'd owned a flat. I

painted the walls and even plumbed in the washing machine (albeit with my dad instructing me on the phone).

But then, despite marrying a twenty-first-century husband, I became a 1950s wife. I took a step back from my glittering career to devote time to my glittering girls, and found myself ground down by the grind. I had built up a new career and was finding my work legs again. But it wasn't the same as before.

Before I had children, my job had been clear and fulfilling. Now, with three small children to care for, my job was a small start-up business that fitted into the gaps of my life when everyone else's needs had been met. I worked when the girls were at school or Montessori and in the evenings when they were in bed. As a great man once said, I never felt I could please all of the people all of the time. Mostly I felt I couldn't please any of the people, any of the time. Something had to be done. Because I was working on all fronts, but nothing was working on my front.

★ ★ ★

Those Sandwich Years, figuring out a work-life balance had taken away my guiding lights and I was often stumbling in the dark. I had to face the fear of the unknown, take a step forward and rediscover who I was. When I became a mum, the shift in gear of my life threw me off my clear direction. It took me down unrecognisable roads and often I couldn't read the signs. I had been so sure of the career girl that the stay-at-home-work-at-home mum stared back at me in the mirror with confused eyes.

When I was first diagnosed with post-natal depression, my GP mentioned that, at some point, I should go for counselling. I had parked that thought along with other plans that seemed impossible from both a mental, emotional and temporal perspective — like just getting on with everyday life. The logistics of getting out of the house by myself to do something as seemingly indulgent as talking about myself made me laugh. I had a young baby, a bedridden mum, a dad who needed support, two small children, a husband and a job. It took me three years after my mother had her stroke to get to the point where: a) I could leave the house without calling in the army and b) my grief had subsided enough for me to be able to speak and the fog had cleared enough for me to think. And the really important thing about counselling is you need to speak and think.

Every time I felt rundown, the GP's words kept coming back to me, whenever I was overwhelmed. Which was still most of the time.

But I felt a fraud. I was doing much better now. I was sad and worn out and put upon but that's life, isn't it? Then something happened that shocked me and I realised that I hadn't improved as much as I'd thought I had.

My girls love to watch themselves on video. They would often sit at the computer and play all the snapshots from the video camera of their early childhood and laugh (and admire) themselves. I walked past them one day and saw a clip of myself bringing in a lit birthday cake to the kitchen. I stopped. I couldn't remember the cake. There was a baby on the floor. Daisy was blowing out the candles. I was looking OK and smiling and had baked a tall pink tower with a sugar-iced Rapunzel leaning out the window. But I couldn't place it.

'Whose birthday is that?' I asked. Daisy looked at me.

'Mine! My fifth!'

I calculated back. That was just four weeks after my mum's stroke. That couldn't be right. Back then I was a dark demon of despair. I Was a gargoyle. The sun had gone in and the world was in darkness, yet this clip was showing light streaming in through the kitchen window. I was laughing and singing. I had washed and put lipstick on. Yet, I had absolutely no memory of that day. And there I was, functioning, performing, being. I'd even baked a pretty cool cake.

Late that night, I crept back downstairs and sat at the computer in the dark and watched my life for the first year after Mum's stroke. There I was. A perfectly functioning human being and I have no recollection of most of the events that were filmed or photographed. My shadow had performed well, so well in fact, I wasn't even there and it really frightened me.

I went back up to bed and lay in the snore-filled darkness and thought about what this meant. It meant one of two things: a) I was so good at putting my face on, I had even fooled myself; or b) I was so mentally ill I had lived a whole other life I knew nothing about (and typically, not one where George Clooney came round and did the dishes).

My GP's words came back to me, and this time I knew I was ready.

Now that I had decided I needed to talk, I had to find someone to listen. I asked around and was recommended CBT counselling. Cognitive behavioural therapy can't change the circumstances of your life, but it can change the way you deal with them. CBT is about identifying and then finding ways to deal in a better way with issues that have, or are, causing you unhappiness, confusion or fear. Finding a counsellor is a bit like going on a dating website — you go online and see their credentials and picture and you choose the one that you think has nice eyes. I researched a few places and made contact with the one friendly face that was near enough to where we lived.

It was pouring with rain when I ran through the door, dripping with winter weather. A bit like my mood. I had no idea what to expect, and no idea if this was a mad idea or a great one. I was also slightly nervous going in, afraid it would all be South American piped filter music and smelly candles. I had a slight fear of having to close my eyes and hum. But when I met Kathleen, she welcomed me in with a smile and took me into a small room with two chairs. No candles. No filtered South American pipe music. Phew! No humming. Double phew! Just a bottle of water and some kind eyes.

I was so nervous. I was worried I had no clear 'problem'. I was worried I would just sound like I was moaning. I was worried I would have nothing specific to say.

I should have worried about how to survive not drawing breath for fifty-nine minutes.

Because I talked solidly for an hour, words gushing out of me, sometimes mingling with tears and sometimes running away by themselves.

Women talk all the time, but this wasn't talking. This was releasing. This was opening a valve and letting off steam I hadn't even realised was building up.

My mum used to have an old thing called a pressure cooker. I don't know if they are even used anymore. It was a big, heavy silver pot she used to make soup in. I'm not exactly sure what difference cooking food under pressure makes (I cook food under pressure all the time, and it doesn't seem to do me much good.) That said, there was, and is, nothing in the world that compares to the emotional nourishment of my mum's lentil soup. It was like drinking a hug in a mug. But this big metal pot would simmer and steam on the stove, and it had a little valve on top that would bubble and squeak and tipple and topple in a pique of agitation. The pot would shake and shudder as the pressure built up inside, and then my mum would shift the valve and steam would funnel furiously out with a relieved squeal.

That was me. That day, I had released the valve.

So many people needed me, but I would be

no use to them if I exploded. That day, I talked about my mum, my dad, my kids, my marriage and, most of all, I talked about me. I realised that in between childcare and parent-care, I had forgotten about self-care. And part of self-care is knowing who that self is.

That first session changed the course of my life.

'I feel like I'm never on top of anything,' I cried.

'That's OK. You don't have to be,' Kathleen said calmly (her voice so much more soothing than any South American piped music).

'But I'm so sad and lost!' I cried.

'I'm not surprised,' she said.

I stopped crying.

'What do you mean?'

She smiled a smile that reached over and took my hand.

'You've experienced a huge amount of pain and stress. You are also trying to live a happy life and be a great mum. It's hard, Alana. Allow yourself to acknowledge what you've gone through. It's perfectly normal for you to be feeling like this.'

'I'm not a failure?'

That smile again.

'Absolutely not. You are struggling, and

why wouldn't you be? You're doing a great job in difficult circumstances. Give yourself a break.'

For someone to tell me that it was OK to be feeling this way was like someone saying, 'You can eat as much chocolate as you like, and you will never get fat.'

It was a gift.

When I became a mum and then a carer, it was as if all the choices of my life had been taken away from me. Counselling helped me to see that there was actually a menu in my life. I couldn't get out of the Sandwich Years, but I could choose what kind of filling I could be, I could choose to have relish. I could choose to have dressing. I could choose. I was also in an increasingly challenging marriage. I was in the conflicting dilemma of having to work and needing to look after my children. I thought I had no choices. But when I started to think about the 'me' in the meaning of life, I realised I had plenty of choice. My mum and I used to sit in my back garden or hers, smiling silently, our faces turned to the sun. When my mum became a shadow, I drifted out of the sunlight. After my first session with Kathleen, I realised I didn't want to live in the shadows anymore. I wanted to live. I was still in the Sandwich Years, but I had emerged from their deep darkness. The light was still faint but, by letting go and reaching out, I had found a torch in my hand. I just needed to figure out in which direction to shine it, to rediscover who I was.

* * *

Counselling really helped me to find my direction again, and decide what I wanted to do and who I needed to be. I had been freelancing for about a year again after Ruby was born but it was scrappy and without any real focus. I began to reclaim my name. Literally. I had gone double-barrelled when I got married, but it never sat well. So as part of deciding what I did and who I was, I decided to stop thinking that all I had was a little meaningless cottage industry and I set up my own business. I gave it a name and took back my own. Double-barrelled emails are not fun. So it made sense to go back to my own name and, in doing so, I also started to go back to me, the person I had always identified with.

I was through the baby years and they had been amazing. But I needed to amaze myself again. I reclaimed my name and I also reclaimed my brain. I took charge of my career. I decided to specialise as a copywriter while pursuing a career in more free-form writing, and not only focus on the creative satisfaction of doing what I loved, but also find a better balance between my children and my work. Sometimes, it was precarious. Sometimes, I tilted too much in one direction. But my arms were outstretched and I learned to walk the line and eventually find my balance.

Most people today struggle with work-life balance, whether or not they have children and parents to care for. The Sandwich Years will throw a big rock on the scales and it's hard to balance anything at all. Between my children, parents and work, I had need hanging off me like piranhas on a screaming swimmer. Even the damn dog was so needy he howled at me when he wanted something and followed me into the toilet.

And it's not even the needs of live things. The fridge beeped at me when I left the door open. The car beeped at me to put my seatbelt on.

The point is, it's hard. I knew enough wonderful women struggling with the same issues as me. How did we find time to do what we loved while doing the other things we loved? To clarify, I mean being with our children was the other thing we loved. I did not mean, and never will mean, the relentless homework that comes with family life. The thinking about what food to give us all, shopping for the food I'd still not thought about, cooking the food without knowing what I was making, washing up the dishes the food was not eaten off, hoovering the food off the floor, and washing the clothes that were covered with the food I'd been fussing over all day.

My girls will have chances I never had. And I had a lot. But will they still be weighed down? Not just by the pressure of the ceiling above them but by the pull of the drudgery below them? How do women manage to find themselves in this fog of family need? How do they find their identity in the web of work demands?

My answer was to try and find elements that reminded me of who I was.

★ ★ ★

I've had many jobs. In my younger years, I've worked in fruit and veg shops, been a waitress and chambermaid (great training for motherhood), barmaid and office maid (sorry, administrative assistant). But my favourite job was as a hotdog girl. Yep. If you ever threw yourself off the 102-metre-high bridge across a ravenous ravine at the Pipeline Bungee in Queenstown, New Zealand sometime in the mid to late 1990s, I probably served you the hotdog that you promptly threw up when you got to the bottom.

For some reason, still inexplicable to me now, I actually threw myself off it a few times too. There you are, all trussed up with what is essentially a thick hair bungee, and every instinct in your body is telling you to stay standing on that platform. *Every* instinct. Because it is much safer up there. And yet, you jump. And it was a thrill. What I learned was that when you cling on, you actually go nowhere and the view always stays the same. But throwing yourself off the ledge altogether is not good for you either. You end up just hanging in midair screaming like an idiot and possibly peeing your pants. No doubt that's the moment George Clooney cruises past on his motorboat to see you suspended upside down crying like a baby.

Letting go is not about falling into the abyss. It is about having the courage to grasp up, and reach out and, hold by hold, step by step, climb back up. But like the bungee, it takes a leap of faith. For many women today, the sheer weight of the work they are expected to carry out outside the home, inside the home, and caring for family makes that reach out seem impossible.

But I've finally worked out the answer.

That is, there is no answer. Just a juggle of challenges, compromises, choices, with a large dollop of guilt and a sprinkling of resentment, all shaken up to make a cocktail of career confusion. It has a slightly bitter taste.

Sometimes we just have to accept that there are a few years of young children and work and parenting that are just hard. That's not a bad thing. It's just a true thing. I'm shouting this bare-breasted, breast-beating again.

IT IS HARD!!!

We are weighed down by responsibility and we don't quite know how to lighten the load. I had found a space to create a place for me, but that didn't mean it was easy. I don't think juggling work and family is ever easy for anyone. Sometimes, you just have to learn to breathe deeply and hopefully get through it. And sometimes you just have to laugh at the ridiculousness of it all.

As a consultant I write about the work of different charities and tell their stories. One of my clients is an overseas medical emergency agency and, last year, I was working on the Ebola crisis for several months. I was asked to interview a particular doctor by phone and, although I usually try and make sure I work when my girls are at school or in bed, sometimes I have to do what suits others. Squeezing in a chat with me between treating Ebola patients trumps my school-run timeframe, so I had to make the call when Ruby was at home. I set her up with her colouring and told her she had to be super quiet.

The line to Sierra Leone isn't great at the best of times. From a makeshift medical tent it's pretty crap, so I had to listen very carefully. This doctor had just spent a day treating children and families dying in their droves from a disease that inflicts maximum indignity and pain. It takes an hour for medical staff just to get out of their protective gear and drink enough water to rehydrate before they collapse into sleep.

When Ruby came into my room to tell me her pen wasn't working I held up that finger — the 'I am working, do *not* disturb' finger — and kept listening and writing.

She persisted. My finger stood strong and then pointed out of the room. She started to wail. I started to run. She followed me. This doctor was telling me about terrible tragedy and I couldn't interrupt him with my domestic issues. So I ran into the downstairs loo and barricaded myself in. Ruby began bashing on the door. I was sitting on the floor, phone in one hand, pen in the other, notebook on my knees, with my feet pushing against the door as she tried to kick it in. Now that I was occupying the toilet, she switched tack, her pens were no longer the issue. 'I want to do a poo!' she screamed. I tried to talk over her noise. I kept asking questions and kept taking notes, the sweat pouring off me. And Ruby shouting 'I want to do a poo!!' more fervently now, every thirty seconds. 'I want to do a poo!' Listen, scribble, sweat. 'I want to do a poo!' I was nearly in tears and not just because of the doctor's story.

At last my call neared its end, and I realised Ruby was no longer screaming. She had stopped kicking the door. I relaxed my feet. I said goodbye. I opened the door. I wished I hadn't. I saw my little girl smiling at me. She pointed to the steaming pile beside her.

'I did a poo.'

My working day.

Many people find that work, home and family are all they have time for. Their options for finding the time for enriching experiences are limited. Most often the problem is money. The glass ceiling has been reached, but many are still pushed under by the class ceiling. But enriching experiences, outside of work, responsibilities and family make up the difference between living and life.

Work was only one part of my journey to finding myself. Others included friends, creativity, exercise, nature, mental stimulation. As we tumbled through the third year and stumbled towards the fourth, there was a period of calm. It no longer felt like I was living in a constant crisis; I was finding myself again.

I began to enjoy things again.

Often, they were little things, like walking my dog or going for a run.

It is very hard to find the time to do things to nourish just ourselves. Sometimes, we need life to hug us, a gesture my mum's lentil soup had perfected. We need its music, culture, art, literature, guilty pleasures, like chocolate. OK, chocolate and gin. The non-guilty pleasures. For me this means books, *The Sunday Times*, baking, reading recipe books (I have fifty-six recipe books and I make the same five dishes, go figure).

What makes people unhappy is powerlessness. Nothing in life is more power-sucking than not being able to do things that make us happy. Slowly, when the girls had settled down in school, and we had settled into a calmer routine with Mum, I began to carve out little bits of time for me. Tiny fragments away from the routine of caring for others, where I cared for myself.

One of those fragments was for running. As well as my dad still running, aged seventy-eight, three times a week, my brother was a long-distance runner. He had long surpassed marathons and had moved on to multi-marathon, multimountain and multi-beyond-me challenges. As a result I was intimidated and never called myself a runner, despite the fact that I had always run. I did 'little' runs but always fought against myself. How a runner can ever say it's lonely I don't know — I was exhausted listening to myself fight with myself over whether I should stop or not, and sometimes I just ran home just to get away from myself.

The farthest I had ever run was the annual Dublin 10 km women's mini-marathon and I just felt that that was my limit. The Dublin marathon runs past our house and, for a few years, we would watch the participants run past in their droves, my girls excitedly handing out waters and bananas. I would fantasise about how one day I would run past, and the girls would run out and cheer me on. Probably George would be there with a quick leg massage and an iced flannel for my sweaty brow.

I started to run a little and it started to make me feel better, although I was convinced I'd never run an actual marathon, but that was OK. It was taking the time out for me that was important.

That, and making sure I occasionally made myself that hug in a mug my mum used to make. I still use her lentil soup recipe, and it always makes me feel comforted:

4 oz red lentils

1.5 pints of ham stock

1 large onion, chopped finely

2 carrots, chopped or grated

Sweat the onions and carrots, then add the lentils and stir well. Add the stock and simmer for 40 minutes.

Put through the blender and serve with crusty bread and a large dollop of love.

8

Seeing Your Supports

Entering the fourth year following my mum's stroke, keeping the juggling balls of my responsibilities in the air while walking the tightrope of my own life had become an everyday reality.

I was still grief-stricken but it wasn't as raw anymore. Life gets in the way of grief. You have to live and grieve and do the dishes and feed your children and whole minutes will go by, and then whole hours, and then even days when you are so busy dealing with the reality of life, the blade of grief stays blunt.

When you become a mother there are no days off. Regardless of how you feel, you still have to be a mother. Just flicking from grief to dishes, from grief to cuddles, from grief to emails, from grief to laughing with your friends, until grief has woven into the fabric of your life like a thread, running through it, stitching all the parts of you together. But also stitched into the fabric of life are the supports we have, and the supports we find. For me, often, it was my supports that got me through; my family, my friends.

From the moment my Sandwich Years began, my friends took up the hand that missed my mum's so much.

Back on that first morning after Mum's stroke, when I walked through the pink bunting of my front door, my best friend Amanda had emerged from the kitchen, having rushed to the house to stay with the girls while my husband took Mum to hospital. Amanda was so much a part of my family that the girls didn't bat an eyelid when they got up in the morning to find her in their parents' bed instead of their dad.

The thing about real friendship is that despite the fact we can talk for twenty hours solid and still feel the need to text later, when tragedy strikes, the best talk is silent. Amanda just put her arms around me. There was nothing to be said. She had tears in her eyes, which I knew were as much for my mum as for me.

Everyone loved my mum. Amanda's reaction was one I would see over and over again. A mirror of my own grief, a reflection of the horror that was happening. For now, I was bruised and broken. My stitches were screaming, and I could barely walk. So Amanda held my arm as I hobbled up the stairs, supporting me like a crutch. I needed to shower and get back to the hospital. Amanda helped me into the bathroom and gently undressed me. I think I just stood there sobbing. When she took off my maternity trousers she stopped pulling. I stopped sobbing. I looked down where she was looking down. I was still wearing the paper pants from the hospital. They are never a good look. But she let this one pass. Tragedy trumps paper pants.

She gingerly pulled their elasticised top away from my C-section wound and pulled them down, my hand on her head. As I had once done with my mum. She stood then and took my arm as I manoeuvred into the shower, and then she hosed me down. Tenderly loving me as my mum had once done. Then she wrapped me in a towel as my mum had done, her friendship a maternal manifestation of love. As I was to discover, despite losing the woman who had been my mum, having many amazing women in my life — Mum's friends and my own — meant I was mothered still.

★　★　★

When I was a little girl, I would look forward to every other Tuesday night. That's when The Girls met in each other's homes. The

Girls consisted of my mum and her friends who had found each other at bus stops and in hospitals all when they were just starting out in married life and having babies.

They had moved into a new 1960s estate and a fully formed community was developed. They wove their lives together, weaving in and out of each other's houses. These Girls became my mum's family and, as a result, they were a part of mine. I called them Auntie Pat and Auntie Hilary and Auntie Margaret and I was loved by each one, very much as if we *were* family. The Girls continued to meet every other Tuesday night for over forty years, and during that epic epoch of sisterhood, they laughed and loved and lamented through every conceivable experience together — marriages, divorces, affairs, children growing, children dying, children getting married, children getting divorced, grandchildren, health scares, financial ruin. It was a soap opera without the credits. Moving house was done as a group effort, as was the decorating afterwards. Together they had holidays, they had parties, they had each other's backs.

I used to love it when it was my mum's turn to host. I would wait up until they all arrived in a flurry of perfume and blue eye-shadow, and then I would sit on the stairs and listen to howls of laughter echo through the lounge door. Sometimes it went quiet, and perhaps these were the times when hushed words of comfort were being handed out with the biscuits. The Girls continued to meet right up until my mum's stroke. Since then, age, death and other inexorable circumstances have diminished the club, but like everything else for those that remain, the most important part still lives. Their love. Ringing some of these Girls to tell them of Mum's stroke had the same effect as ringing my brother.

My mum was their family and I knew it was going to devastate them.

And it did.

But they knew what I still had to learn. You keep going and you make the best of Plan B. I don't think I understood until then the depth of their friendship, or the responsibility they would take on themselves to help us care for Mum. I still have the text from Pat: 'I have known your Mum for forty years. I will always do anything for her.' And she, and others, have.

They have been a constant presence in our lives since my mum's stroke. In a funny way, they do still meet as The Girls, coming to my mum's house every other Monday night now to allow my dad to go out — with 'The Boys', average age: eighty-three. They sit with Mum, they do her hair and paint her nails. They bring her presents and love. She has no memories to draw on to go with their faces, but she has all that matters. Her love. Her face lights up when she sees them. She may not remember their names, but she remembers that she loves them. When everything else is gone, love remains.

And that love extends in a chain to me and to my daughters. They have become my mum-in-situ, and have made me an honorary member of The Girls. They sit with my mum, and hold her hand and talk to her and love her still. And now they also do it for me. My mum's other best friend, Evelyn, who lives in the UK is the same. She rings me now as my mum would have done, and we share the ups and downs of our lives. She is there for me, as she was there for my mum. And all of them treat my girls like grandchildren, showering their love on them on behalf of my mum. I could no longer have my Plan A. So my mum's friends stepped up to garnish my Plan B.

As I grew up and started exploring adult life, I often felt a sort of jealousy for The Girls. That tight unit of friendship seemed unlikely to happen to me as I scattered myself around the world, going to university here, working there, travelling everywhere. The

Girls came about from one period of time and one area. But I soon realised I was gathering mine up along the way.

When I finally settled in Dublin, my own group of friends settled too. In many aspects of life, from work to travel to the school gates, I have an army of women who battle alongside me, celebrating my victories and crying with me on my losses. I don't have The Girls that meet every other Tuesday night — but I have My Women. Amazing women friends who get me through the day, and make me laugh into the night. A weird and wonderful group of strong and sassy women from all walks of my life.

It was to these friends that I turned. I had to ask for help and I had to start being strong. In honour of my mum and all that she taught me, with the help of her friends, my family and my friends, and after the support of counselling I would get up and take a step forward. I had witnessed the power of friendship as the mainstay of my mum's life, and they have become the mainstay of mine.

My mum used to say, 'I'd be lost without my friends.' And it wasn't until the Sandwich Years that I realised this wasn't a throwaway cliché. It meant at times they shone a torch when there was no other light, and helped me map-read when the lines of life blurred. As the intensity of the Sandwich Years drained me of colour, it was my friends who threw paint splashes on my washed-out canvas. Work provided a space for me to find a creative outlet. Friendships provided a place for me to find an outlet for *me*. A place where I was not a mother or a wife or a daughter or a writer. A place where I was just me, and loved and appreciated for that.

This is not a list of names on Facebook or Instagram. When the chips are down, these are the names who will turn up at your door without being asked because they know you should have asked, and whose call you will take at 10 p.m. just when you are settling down with a packet of Doritos and a glass of wine to watch some trash TV and switch off.

Roxane Gay, in her essay, 'How To Be Friends with Another Woman', describes her mother's favourite saying: 'Qui se ressemble s'assemble.' It means, essentially, you are whom you surround yourself with. I learned from my mum to surround myself with the best people I knew, and that has made all the difference to my life.

For over ten years, I have attended a book club and, at times, it was my only social life. But we would gather around a table, a mismatch of women as different and interesting as the books we read, and we would open ourselves up like pages and talk about life, our problems, our dramas, and very occasionally the actual books. I have reached an age where I don't want meaningless conversation. I want gritty, crunchy, meaningful conversation, and if it has to be frivolous, at least it should be with gritty, crunchy, meaningful friends.

Over these ten years, the soundtrack to my life has been speckled with the cackles of laughter alongside the rub of fabric, as our arms have embraced. My friends have cried in my arms, and I have cried in theirs. My friends have talked hours of unbelievable shit and they have listened to hours of mine. My friends have picked me up off the floor, and I have carried them home. Frankly, I would not have survived the Sandwich Years, or my life, without them. Making time for this piece of me was one of the most important things I did. Seeing my mum as a woman outside of being my mum was such an important lesson in seeing her as a person with a life. I think that helped us in those middle years between my dependence on her, and her dependence on me — through her 'Girls', I was able to see her not just as a wife and mother, but as a real person who was loved because of who she was, not what she was.

I want my daughters to see that they are

loved by the family they are born into and form, but that they will also be loved by the family they create for themselves, through friends. They need to see me as a person so that they know that despite all the labels they will become, they will always be themselves first. And like my mum's friends became my family, so my close friends are my children's family. They will be there for them when my girls can't (or won't) speak to me. They will mother them alongside me, because they are the sisters I would have chosen and the family I created.

The family I was born into also gave me life-saving support too. The family we are from gives us a place in a story. I know my mum's life inside out. She regaled us with so many stories of her childhood I often wondered why I was missing from the grainy black-and-white photos she would show me.

From the earliest days of her stroke, as she lay in a bed unable to recognise the people in those albums, it became my job to now tell her the story of her life. Mum always talked about her childhood. She talked about her kind old dad, Jimmy. She talked about her mum, the raven-haired girl called Gypsy, the woman I only knew as a big-bosomed, white-haired Nanna Kilgore who made mince taste good.

Mum took comfort in the past, it helped to reassure her, ground her, and I realised how important that is only when I faced my own mid-life shock.

When I was growing up, upstairs on the landing, we always had a little rogues' gallery of black-and-white photos — my grandparents as young people, my great-grandparents and other family members, grainy grey faces hanging in the shadows of my everyday life. As a child, I would often stop and gaze at them, wondering what they were like. They looked so static and unreal. I would try to imagine them moving and talking. Now, in my own home, I have the same rogues' gallery, and we have added new colour pictures as the family generations descend; our parents, us, our children. And I still often stop and stand at the wall, looking deeply into those long-gone faces, wondering at the lives lived, lives now lost, lives entwined. I wonder how they had felt, and what they had thought, as I feel and think my way through life's obstacle course. Did they think the same thoughts as me? Did they feel the same fears?

I knew snippets of their lives, seemingly so different to mine . . . and yet. They *are* mine. Their experiences led to me. Their genes are in me. Decisions they made affected the socio-economic imprint of my life, their behaviours and loves affected the colour of my eyes. It makes me feel a part of something, that I have heritage behind me as I try to leave a legacy after me.

I remember sitting on the bottom of my nanny and pappa Kirk's bed, enthralled by his stories of himself as a mischievous boy. My mum would tell me stories of her exploits growing up, and I knew the colour and style of every dress she had going to 'dances' when she was a young single woman. And when I look at that wall, all that is left of them is their stories. And the love they passed down. The love we pass down is the only real legacy.

As I continued to care for my mum above and my daughters below, with me on the middle branch of this family tree, I realised that life wasn't the cycle that so many people talked about, it was a chain, each piece individual but linked, just like my charm bracelet.

I spent many hours wholly focused on trying to get my mum back. I would sit beside her bed and go through the photos, pointing out people and places, but she rarely seemed to recognise them. I showed her all our family photos, reminded her of the times we had shared. She would smile and say, 'Oh yes!' but her eyes told the truth. Those moments were all forgotten. It was devastating. A lifetime of love and memories wiped out in a stroke of the clock.

I know that for many people, this is one of the hardest parts of losing a parent, whether it happens in an instant or memories seep away over time like a leaking pipe. It really upset me that the people she had talked about so much, and the times we had spent together, no longer meant anything. But gradually I realised that they did. The memories might have gone, but we weren't strangers. She couldn't remember the times or places, but she could remember how she felt. When everything else was gone, all that was left was the love.

She knew us all, her face lighting up when she saw us, but she couldn't say (or remember) our names. The only name she could remember, and say, was my dad's.

People talk nowadays about the importance of living in the now, that the present is the only place to be. Well my mum was reduced to just the present. She no longer had a past, and she could no longer think about the future. All she lives every day was every moment, and it was a terrible place to be. We need the past to make sense of the present, and we need the future to guide us. Living in the now was not living at all. And the only thing that made it bearable was the only thing that is really left behind, the heritage of love.

★ ★ ★

For me, that love tastes of lipstick. When I was a child, I didn't like getting my face wet, which was unfortunate when I was in a swimming pool. I remember one Wednesday evening when chlorine stung my eyes and echoing screams splashed around my ears. It was family swim night at the local pool. I was struggling to finish the length when I spotted my mum. She was swimming in the shallow end, her head lifted high above the water, not a wet hair on her head. She didn't like getting her face wet either. So she swam like a movie star, gentle breast stroke, her head lifted above the water, her lipstick still intact. A sort of Belfast Audrey Hepburn. She waved at me and then opened her arms to invite me to swim to her. I surged forward until I was there in her hug and she gave me a kiss.

I had to do ten more lengths and so I set off again for the deep end, but the taste of her lipstick stayed on my lips and as I struggled to the top I licked them again and again, each lick of lipstick giving me a little more strength. Every two lengths I got another lipstick reward and, each time, the taste kept me going until my next one. My mum's lipstick rewards took many forms over the years, in hugs, in calls and in letters.

If love tastes of lipstick, it smells of tissue-thin blue airmail paper. Letters of love have filtered through my life as regular and as essential as the seasons. I love letters. I still write them. I rarely receive them now that my mum can't write, but my whole life, her handwriting appeared through my varied front doors to remind me I was loved. Though my mum no longer writes to me, my bedside drawer is now filled with love notes from my daughters. Almost as soon as Mum stopped, they began, the chain chinking that background melody of continuity.

My mum started writing to me when I was eighteen and went to teach English in a school in Pakistan on my gap year. I would wait for the little blue envelopes to bring me glimpses of my home. Thin paper thick with news. The world was bigger than I had ever imagined and I wanted to see it all but, over the years, home always came with me in the form of a blue envelope. Mum's neat and perfect loops and curls did not just bring her words to me. They brought me back home. I loved being in Pakistan. I loved the spice-stained air, and the hot-headed breath of the heat. I loved the gentleness of the people and drama of the streets. But I loved those letters too, so flimsy in weight, yet heavy with the thought put into them.

My mum always used to say, 'It's great going away', but then she would look at me and smile, 'But it's even better coming home.' I now say it to my girls and they say it back to me because we know it's true.

She wrote to me all through my gap year and I wrote back. Letters filled with shock and awe and drama, letters that made me reflect on my experiences. When I returned, tanned with the sun of adventure, I went to university in England. She wrote to me every week there too. I probably didn't write back every week, but I did write.

My knowledge was growing and my scope was widening, as I pulled farther and farther away from my family life of dependence, and farther and farther towards my own life of independence. But her letters always sent me a little bit of home. She didn't just send me words. She once sent me a birthday cake in the post to my digs in university. A whole cake. With chocolate icing. In the post. Sometimes a letter just isn't enough. Love is many things, but most definitely it is a chocolate cake in the post.

Our letters weren't just paper, they were love letters of memory, moments saved for a time when there would be no more envelopes in the post.

Sometimes the love lingered long after they were written. When I drove up to Belfast one weekend, I found a big box my dad had lugged down from the attic and left in my room. I looked inside, and found my life story.

The smell of age and nostalgia mingled with tissue-thin paper and ink. Every single card, every single letter, every single postcard, every single note I had ever written to my mum was inside . . . stories laid bare, love notes squeezed between exploits, happy holidays, dull days . . . all bound together in a memory bundle of paper. I had written to my mum all through my life — through my adventures, through my education, through my relationships, through my parenting. And she'd kept every word.

I spent a few hours just putting them into piles — the piles that represent the phases of my life. My childhood — sweet notes of innocence and a burgeoning imagination; my gap year in Pakistan and India as a naive eighteen-year-old — full of longing for home, and excitement at the world; university — an adult emerging amid learning and independence; working life in London — lots of money requests and false starts on the job front; my two-year travels — the splendour, the adventure, the romance!; and finally, Dublin — my first flat, planning our wedding, our first home, my beautiful girls.

Reading them, I realised how honest I was with Mum, how at ease we were with each other, how accepting we were, how involved my parents have been in my life.

Not only did that box give me a unique diary of my forty years on this planet, it was like a gift to me as I grieved for my mum, and learned to live without her involvement. Her handwriting was always a waving reminder that whatever else I was doing, I had a home. So I decided to continue that tradition and I started to write to her again. I typed out letters and embedded photos of my girls and emailed them to Dad. He would print them off and read them to her. She wasn't able to read them herself, but she held them, and looked at the photos and that was enough. They are slowly filling a box beside her bed — and in time too they will become the diary of this phase, and a reminder that even though she cannot be the person she was, she is still, and always will be, involved in my life.

And I write to my girls. Letters that they don't read yet, but will open in a box some day. The letters will be the diary of their childhood and maybe, just maybe, give them a base to jump off into adulthood. I hope I'll still be writing to them through every phase of their lives, and I hope some day, no matter where they are or what they are doing, my words will be a waving reminder that they always have a home and a family.

★   ★   ★

During those first few years after Ruby's birth and mum's stroke, the two breads of my sandwich pushed me to my limits. I was stretched so thin, I couldn't be seen as a filling. Yet time and time again, those breads also wrapped me in their love, making me not only a filling but a filling with relish. I was part of something extraordinary. A club sandwich. A club I was happy to be a member of, part of a chain, part of the past and part of the future. The future can't exist without the past, and often I have struggled with managing the two forceful elements of my life — the pre-children and post-children me. The me that thought she knew everything and who realised she knew nothing. In her years of good health, my mum was the bridge between the two, keeping me sane and intact while I often unravelled. All through my teenage and early adult life, my mum had shouted frustrated and frustratingly at me,

'Just you wait. Just wait until you have kids and you'll see how hard this is', and I would roll my eyes. Now, when the demands of the girls threaten to overwhelm me, my raised eyebrow and my rolled eyes say just one thing: *She was right.*

It would not be an understatement to say it had been a struggle. Seven pregnancies, three children under six, and several life-changing events, untold dramas, adventures and crises. And let's not forget the mundane — the endless, endless, endless, endless, endless, endless meals to be planned, bought for, prepared, fed, coerced-fed, force-fed, washed up, wiped up; the countless, countless, countless, countless nights of vomiting, crying, nightmares, wet beds, the howls of 'I want a hug and I don't care that it's 3 a.m.'; the various hideous child-related tasks that no-one warns you about — lice, worms, leaking nappies, leaking nappies that defy belief as the shit creeps up their back and down their arms, children who walk slower than a snail; the relentless, relentless, relentless picking up of other people's clothes, because three girls like to change outfits multiple times per day. And they weren't even teenagers!

But as the nappy smell started to fade and the little people started to grow, there were glimpses of proper payback. We talk about the thankless job of motherhood — but, you know what? Accepting that it's thankless is just I'm-so-sorry-for-being-a-woman talk. I'd like thanks occasionally. While it's a job I'm very thankful to have, must it be a thankless one?

Mothers should be appreciated by their partners, society and government for the amazing job they do. I'd like a salary and a company car, please. OK, I'll settle for a back rub. I'm ready to enjoy the perks and forget the downers. All those nappies? Nearly forgotten. All those wretched meals left uneaten? Almost forgotten. All those early mornings? Forgotten. Why? Because the chain was still chinking.

One night, with no warning, life gave me a present. Just like my mum would brush my hair and I would rub her back, Daisy decided to give me a foot rub with baby lotion, while Poppy brushed my hair. We have regular girlie nights now, and moments when we just pamper each other, laugh and do nice things for each other, as I had done with my mum. As I do with my mum still, rubbing her with face cream, brushing her hair and putting on her makeup. All of us wrapped in a chain. What goes around, comes around.

For years, my mum wiped my bum and

soothed my teeth and caught my vomit and sat up worrying. It's payback time. I'm happy to pay it all back. She did so much for me, this is what I want to do for her. There is a certain comfort that comes with knowing that payback is due. Every time a child of mine has a tantrum and sends me to Planet Pissed Off, I smile and think about my later years of flatulence and fungus. Of that one glamorous time I chased a diarrhoea-spilling daughter up the stairs and fell flat on my face in it. That child owes me at least a few corn removals. That's the chain of love. We don't do it because we have to, but because we want to.

Part of being big is to remember and teach the small people their heritage. That they are part of something. That they have the supports they are born into as well as the ones they create. To show them where they come from so they can decide where they want to go. All my life I have asked my parents and grandparents and other family to tell me stories, because their stories intrigued me so much. And now the girls ask me constantly to tell them a story. The chain continues.

As I rack my brains, they prompt me to tell them about when I was a little girl. And I lie on their beds beside them as Mum did with me, stroking their long hair as Mum did with me, and I tell them about eating so much chocolate one Easter that I threw up buckets of brown vomit all night. I tell them about my rabbit who nearly bit my dad's finger off. I tell them about the elephant that chased us in Africa when I was a child.

'You were chased by an elephant, Mummy?' they ask wide-eyed.

'I was,' I boast.

I tell them about walking a rehabilitated orangutan through the jungles of Borneo. 'You held their hand, Mummy?'

'I did.'

And I tell them of many, many, many other adventures and excitements and experiences, many in faraway lands, that have made my life incredible. And in telling them, I suppose I relived them again. And I realised that while they had their whole life ahead of them, and my mum was nearing the end of hers, I only have half of mine behind me. It is a map littered with roads and avenues explored and enjoyed. And hopefully I have another half yet to live, more paths to travel, unknown and unexplored, and the difference is that now there are lots of footsteps walking alongside mine.

And so I knew I had to keep going. I would look at the photo albums and be reminded that I must keep making my life — now theirs and hers — extraordinary.

* * *

It is only through support that we can survive momentous times. My friends and my family carried me through, but so did people I had never met. I have always loved writing, even as a child. From angst-ridden teen diaries, to love-riddled adult journals, I used words as solace. And through my blogging, shared experiences in this challenging situation with my online sisterhood brought me love and laughter and comfort and strength.

Discovering I was not alone, that I wasn't supposed to be sailing through this, that others understood what I was going through, that the resilience was there in me, helped me through some of the darkest days. These people I'd never met helped shine a light on it when my mum was unable to. And that army of women around me, with my own friends at the frontline, kept me protected from the onslaught of stress.

I knew there had been armies of women before me doing the very same. Blogging is a modern phenomenon, but long before the internet, the concept of asking for support, of sharing experiences, of giving comfort certainly existed. This is how communities have operated throughout the ages. As modern life brought women opportunities to grow and flourish, it also brought them isolation and despair. We left our communities to see the world, so new communities had to be found. One such new-found community inspires me still. It started with someone asking for help. Literally.

In 1935, an advertisement appeared in the UK's *The Nursery World* magazine, perhaps the pre-war version of *Grazia*. The ad simply said: 'Can Any Mother Help Me?'

In those days, women gave up their jobs when they married, and raising a handful of kids with little support from husbands was the norm. The woman who had placed the advertisement was desperately lonely and isolated, and needed creative interaction. She got so many replies from so many women around the country they decided to set up their own secret magazine. They all took anonymous names and wrote articles about their lives that were printed in a magazine that ran on subscriptions and a small print run. It would start with one woman and one article and it would be posted to the next, who read it and then added another article. She would then post it on to the next name on the list and on it went until every member had read and written in that issue. They eventually had several issues on the go simultaneously. Through their child-rearing years, through the Second World War, through marriage breakdowns and life's highs and lows, these women found comfort in their writing and their friendships. The magazine — titled *Co-operative Correspondence Club (CCC)* — lasted for over fifty years.

These women's lives were often harsh, and many had been educated but forced to become nothing more than domestic drudges after marriage. They endured bringing up their children alone and in austere circumstances during the war and they fought their own battles to find identity, creativity and achievement. They were brave, funny, witty, enduring, strong and smart. They worked much longer and much harder than I do, and they still found time to write.

Until the CCC disbanded in 1990, these women literally wrote the story of their lives, wielding a weapon against boredom, domestic drudgery, marriage and motherhood. Life gave them something to write about, and writing gave their life meaning. And so it gave mine. My blog not only acted as a therapy session (and was free), but it formed a community around me of women who, like me, needed and gave support to each other. Through the blog I also realised that most of what I wrote about was not the filling (me), but the bread that supported me — my mum and my children. They were the strength on the outside, keeping me together. Different ends of the spectrum. Same chain of love.

★   ★   ★

When Mum first had her stroke, I thought I had to learn to live without her support. But I realise now that her support was always with me. Poppy danced in her first ballet show. Daisy wrote stories and discovered the delight of her own voice through song, and Ruby was full of wonder for life. We had adventures, we made plans, we lived our days, and my mum missed it all. And we were missing her. I knew that no-one would have devoted more time to sitting on the sofa hearing Daisy read than she would have. I knew she would have started to write letters to Daisy, and would have enjoyed getting replies. I knew she would have listened avidly as a younger Poppy regaled tales of her imaginary friend, Heart. I knew Ruby would be wearing little dresses that Mum would bring down ('I just couldn't help myself'), and she'd be bending the ears of everyone she knew with Ruby's minxy antics.

My mum had taught me many things. How to bake. How to sew. How to knit. How to make pavlova. She had even tried to teach me how to stack a dishwasher. And as I imparted my knowledge on a daily basis to the girls, I started to pass on many of those skills. As I poured the cake-mix into the tin, little voices squealed for me to leave some in, their hands already delving into the bowl, their faces smeared with chocolate goo. A flashback. My face. Mum smiling as she passed me the bowl and put another cake in the oven.

Four years after Mum's stroke, as I made some Christmas presents, sewing on buttons to some egg cosies, Daisy asked me to teach her and so I handed her the needle and thread and guided her to push it in, and pull it through. A flashback. Mum making my dress for my first formal dance, allowing me to sew on a few stitches.

A lazy Saturday morning, three little heads would peer around the bedroom door, and seeing me awake, leap onto the bed and snuggle under the duvet with me, chirping and chattering. More flashbacks. An uncountable number of mornings lying beside my mum under her duvet, putting the world to rights. As an adult as well as a child.

While I dealt with the disintegration of my relationship with my mum, I was building a new relationship with my girls in her memory. She was still always there. Her hands on mine, folding in the cake mix, pushing through the thread, holding up a book in bed, stroking long hair. Even years on, I was still shocked by what had happened. On those long afternoons in Belfast, she lay downstairs, bedbound and trapped, while I wandered around her bedroom upstairs, her things still as she had left them. Her clothes still hung in the wardrobe. She had bought many of them with me on one of our outings, but I knew she would never wear them again. It was easier now to dress her in loose-fitting sweat pants and jumpers. Her jewellery glistened in the drawer, each piece with a story. She would never wear most of the pieces again, only a few select simple earrings and necklaces. Her photos, her books, her mementos of life scattered around her old room like moments in time. She would never be up there to touch them again. And I realised what her most important lesson had been. That none of those things mattered. What mattered was in me. My mum had always felt insecure about not finishing school or having a big career or any official 'accomplishments'. Yet, everyone who knew her, loved her. Everyone. She invested her time in people. She gave her love out like sweets. She touched people, literally and emotionally.

When I look back on all the things I have learned — from school, from university, from night courses, from reading — I realise that actually the only things I learned that really count are the things I have learned from her: how to love, how to be kind, how to value your friends. She didn't have a degree but she had a philosophy: people matter. She always made people matter.

I didn't know now how to carry on without her, but at least I had that. Mum had always put herself down about her lack of education, but what she didn't perhaps realise was that the things that make a person great are not a list of accomplishments or a long CV. At the end of the day, as these years had shown me, the only thing that matters, the only thing that determines greatness, is the love you leave behind. And if the love we leave behind is the greatest accomplishment of all . . . then my mum was the most accomplished person I knew.

★   ★   ★

Like my mum, I love lists. And like she wrote a list about me, I've written a list about some of the things my mum taught me:

— Earl Grey tea should always be drunk with a little bit of something nice.

— With friends and family, always be the bigger person and say sorry, even if it's not really your fault (this really pisses them off and makes them feel rubbish when it is theirs — and very loved).

— Always make an effort to put your face on. Not for anyone else but yourself.

— Cover your cleavage.

— Lists are essential for living.

— Baking bowls are for licking.

— Holidays are not holidays without a Tupperware box full of goodies.

— Never give up or let yourself go.

— You are never too old for a cuddle with your mum.

— Friends are the mainstay of your life.

— There is only one thing more important than family and friends. Love.

— Always turn your face to the sun.

And why stop at one list? Here's a list for my girls:

— When you've had three children, don't jump on the trampoline unless you've gone to the toilet first and emptied your bladder.

— If you have cleavage, show it off. What the hell (but only after the age of twenty-five, please, girls).

— Love your lists and know that long after your friend's designer handbag is out of fashion, your stationery shop blow-out will still be serving you well.

— Baking bowls are for licking.

— Make sure your partner appreciates you.

— Be honest.

— You're never too old to get into bed with me for a cuddle.

— Be kind to others, but especially to yourself.

— Friends are the mainstay of your life.

— Always turn your face to the sun (but put factor 50 on first, you don't want my age spots).

— Choose happiness.

9

Adapting to Plan B

While limbo grief is really hard, and letting go and accepting a new situation can be extraordinarily painful, it also has a positive element. Accepting and adjusting to new circumstance enables you to embrace the changes and make the best of what is probably a very bad situation. For years after Mum's stroke I lived in a constant time warp. I still hankered after the past, I still lurched from one moment to the next, trying to keep the present moving (and my girls alive), and the future was some point 'out there' that I kept working towards, a point when the kids could all tie their own shoelaces and make me a meal, and when George Clooney could come around to hang up the washing in the garden.

I have lots of amazing women in my life whom I love. Some I share wine, wit and wisdom with, and some I've never met. Sheryl Sandberg is one of my unmet heroines. Not just because of her path-breaking TED talk or her first book *Lean In* which champions the strength of women in the workplace. It was the way she demonstrated her strength in the deepest grief that really touched me. She lost her husband, suddenly, tragically and when she wrote about her grief on Facebook a month later, it was quite profound. Part of what she said really resonated with me.

> *I think when tragedy occurs, it presents a choice. You can give in to the void, the emptiness that fills your heart, your lungs, constricts your ability to think or even breathe. Or you can try to find meaning. These past thirty days, I have spent many of my moments lost in that void. And I know that many future moments will be consumed by the vast emptiness as well.*

> *But when I can, I want to choose life and meaning.*

You don't want to let go. You don't want to let go! I did not want to acknowledge or accept my mum was gone in the sense of who she had been. It was utterly, utterly undoable. It's hard to start climbing back up when you can only cling on for dear life, but when you cling on, you never move. You either cling on forever or your fingers seize up with cramp and you simply drop off into the abyss. To reach up, you have to let go of one hand. In her Facebook post Sheryl Sandberg told how one day she cried to a friend that she still wanted her husband to do a sports event with her child. He told her simply, 'Option A is not available. So we are going to kick the shit out of Option B.'

I'm a planner. I used to plan my plans. My friends would borrow the colour-coded baby charts for sleeping and eating that had adorned my fridge doors. I even had a spreadsheet on the computer on which I'd designed a checklist for going out with the babies. (I know, I know!)

Plan A had been to raise my children with my mum walking alongside me, tutting at my dishwasher-stacking skills and teaching me songs. Giving out to me for doing everything at warp speed, then sitting me down for a cup of Earl Grey and a little bit of something nice. But Plan A was no longer available. It got trampled on in the rush of life events I had no control over. I knew I had to let go of it and the pain of that was extraordinary. Especially when it felt like a betrayal. I could still hold Mum's hand and look in her eyes, sit beside her and drink tea. So it was hard to let go of still wanting all that we had had. But she could no longer say, 'Oh, let's have a little bit of something nice,' so I would say it for her.

As I let go of who she had been, instead of resisting everything, I started to accept that we must do new things. I could still tell her all about my life and my girls, and she could still smile. I could bring the girls to see her and watch her face light up. They could snuggle into her bed and instead of her reading them stories, they could read her stories. I could sit beside her and sip Earl Grey and show her pictures. Her friends could come around and share time, wine, memories, laughs and love. The unbearable darkness had become slightly more bearable. I had started to learn to take life as it comes — as my mum had always taught me — and make the best of what I had. I may have been ready to say goodbye to Plan A, but I still hadn't figured out what Plan B would be. The thought of it was frightening, stepping into the unknown.

After the first year, my mum had improved a little and my family had worked as a team to try and make things as bearable as we could. I had supplied the emotional uplift for Mum, while Dad and Simon were the practical side of the operation. Dad had made his ramps and pullies and kept on making meals. Simon came up with solid, material ways to make things more bearable. Imagine the science-head nerdy boy who made things out of Meccano and took things apart and put them back together. That was my brother. He might have been a hippy but he always came up with a plan. After the stroke, Mum couldn't stand, so once she was hoisted into the chair, she was stuck there until she could be hoisted back out when the carers came back to change her four or five hours later. Often the time she was in the wheelchair became a bit frustrating for her and for us. During the second year my brother had been the bravest first. He had ordered a special taxi that could accommodate a wheelchair and he took her out for lunch. Mum had left the house! Soon after I took that momentous step and I remember how it felt to be able to walk around a shopping centre and have lunch out. We ordered Earl Grey tea and, yes, had a little bit of something nice to go with it.

In the second year, Mum had had the peg in her stomach removed because she no longer needed to have her food pumped into her; this had made a great difference. She ate real meals which my dad valiantly cooked every day. She could talk, although she would never regain cognitive function and was often very confused. She was still paralysed and doubly incontinent. But she could still give out to us all, which made us feel at home. This was Plan B.

And after we'd had that first taste of freedom, there had been no holding us back. Taxis were too expensive and restrictive, so Simon had located a second-hand van that had been adapted to take a wheelchair passenger in the back. And so the 'Pat-mobile' arrived. (Yes my mum has an actual name other than Mum. It is Pat.) The Pat-mobile changed our lives. I was able to take my three kids and Mum out for the day. We were able to leave the house. Go actual places, where my children could run around and my mum could be part of it. Ruby sat on Mum's knee on the wheelchair instead of me performing the ridiculous farce of pushing the wheelchair with one hand and one hip, while pushing her buggy with one hand and one foot. That first day we got out — albeit after doing the fourteen straps to get Mum tied in, and three children in child seats — I rolled down the window and shouted out 'Freeeeedoooom!!!'. Brave-hearted and happy-hearted.

We were starting to sprinkle some glitter on Plan B and it was more bearable than I had expected. That doesn't mean that Plan B didn't entail taxing days. Days when my mum couldn't connect. Days when she was in terrible pain. Days when her bodily functions stripped her of dignity. As time went on there were days she was so depressed she begged me to make it all stop. 'I don't want this,' she would whisper, clasping my hand. But Plan B also did give us good days and good weekends. It even had good weeks. But it was always a pull.

The logistics of managing a busy household with three small children (two of school age, one a toddler) with a husband who worked long hours, and a career I was trying to build while getting up to see Mum and give Dad a break, were still pretty brutal. I still had a heavy feeling in my stomach when I looked at the calendar. All those weekends marked out away from family life staring at me. Occasionally there were whole blocks of four or five days marked out. Weeks when my brother took my dad away for a break, and I needed to stay with Mum. In the months leading up to one of these, the dread would sit in my stomach. Days away from my girls! But my focus was on finding childcare, school pick-ups and making meals for the freezer. The childcare sometimes came in the form of my husband's fabulous aunt who travelled over from Uganda to look after three young tearaways and change her first nappies at the age of sixty. But eventually, as the squeals of delight of my three daughters greeted me down the phone every day, I would relax into the time with my mum.

In the months immediately after her stroke, I had never thought I'd enjoy my time with her again. She'd been a shadow. And I'd been scared of her strangeness. But once I had embraced Plan B, it all became a little easier.

I did her hair and makeup every day, and we laughed. Really laughed. She had improved so much that, at times, I forgot the fear and enjoyed the fun.

I took her out to the shopping centre and around the park in the sun. Her friends came for lunch and stayed all afternoon. We watched and sang to *The Sound of Music* (OK, I sang) and went through old photos. She still couldn't remember people or names, but she engaged nonetheless. Every morning, I brought a little table in beside her bed, and worked beside her on my laptop, chatting and drinking tea. Mostly she slept, so I was able to work. And in the evenings, I would hop up on her bed and lie beside her while we watched TV. For the odd time like that, I almost had my mum back.

In the months after my mum's stroke, I had been horrified and harrowed by having to tend to the same needs of two people at the opposite ends of life. There had come a sudden ream of tasks I had had to perform while also nursing my daughter. Changing Mum's pad, spoon-feeding her pureed food, figuring out what she was trying to say. And even when her speech did become clear, she was more than often confused and unable to articulate her feelings and thoughts. Four years on so much had changed, despite so much being the same. My mum could now talk and feed herself, albeit in a limited way. Ruby could now talk and feed herself, albeit in her own way.

One day a momentous thing happened for them both. My daughter completed her first jigsaw — and so did my mum. It was a jigsaw I'd had made for Mum, from a picture of the girls. It was the first time either had the concentration span, the cognitive intelligence and the skills to complete a puzzle.

The previous few years had been an awakening for them both. Ruby was leaving the baby years behind and becoming a proper little person, communicating more effectively, being funny and engaged. My mum had been making more sense, recognising pictures of her own mother, Gypsy. We could laugh together again sometimes. And one day I decided we would bake again. I made the dough and rolled it out and with her one good hand, she pressed the cutter, my hand on hers to keep it steady. My mum had taught me to bake, as I now teach my children. It was something we always did together and this day I got to do it again. Ruby joined in and together, my mum, my daughter and I made biscuits.

We walked the dog in the autumn sunshine and, later, we had a pretend tea party. Mum and Ruby laughed and connected — something I never dreamed could happen in those awful, awful months after her stroke. And while it was still more difficult for Daisy and Poppy, who remembered Nanna so well from before her stroke, it was the little things like laughing and baking together that made the biggest difference.

Those days as I cared for Mum, I was spending so much time in my childhood house that it had that old familiar feel. Yet it was strange. Because no matter how old I got or how independent I became, I always shrank down when I walked through that front door, the child returning. But here I was, learning to be a parent to my parent, while the daughter in me roamed in her childhood footsteps.

I was no longer the random visitor I had been for the previous twenty years, dumping my rucksack on the floor on my way in, and leaving my breath on the window pane on my way out. Instead, I was now leaving my imprint in the bed every other weekend, my things accumulating in bedside drawers and wardrobes once again. Pyjamas, underwear, makeup, shampoo. I had my own home now, with my own children, but I would always be a child of this home. The Sandwich Years made me the child and the parent entwined.

As my mum lay downstairs, I would wander the rooms of my adolescence and touch the memories as I ran my hands over the walls. Fights, laughs, chats. The front door opening and closing a thousand times as I went to and from school. Now I wheeled Mum in and out, and wheeled a pram in and out and my kids ran in and out chasing my childhood ghost around the house. I remembered the hours I'd spent standing in the hallway talking on the phone to friends and shy first kisses at the front door. The whispers my bedroom walls heard as I revised for exams, wrote secrets in my diary, gazed beyond the horizon and imagined how my life would unfold. Now I could sit at the table again, working, trying to fit my work life into my care life and parenting life. I'd spent hours beside my mum, licking baking bowl spoons in the kitchen, or on the sofa learning the lessons of my life. Now I baked again with that same mixer, and used those same bowls.

Back where it all began, trying to figure out how to put those lessons to use.

* * *

As we neared the end of the fourth year, a subtle shift began to take place. We had spent three years focusing on the crisis around Mum. But slowly my eyes turned away and I saw my dad standing in the wings, and I realised that he too needed much more caring for. Being her full-time carer was beginning to take its toll.

Dad is a proud and capable man. He is also a medical phenomenon. He drinks only strong black coffee, wine and whiskey. If you produced a glass of water for him, he'd throw it on a pot plant. Yet he was still climbing mountains and running three times a week.

When Mum's stroke threw our family into disarray, the new dynamics of family rearrangement took a while to negotiate. Dad had always been the boss of our family. No questions asked. But he had gradually mellowed over the years and our family had taken on a more democratic hue. Still, after Mum's stroke, figuring out the dynamics of caring for him while still enabling him to be a parent to us was a challenge. There were plenty of times we clashed. I became a regular weekend visitor. My mum had been the talker, my dad the quiet man, not one for idle chit-chat. But here he was, having carers come into his home six times a day for Mum, and his children descending on him every weekend. And in my case, often with three children and a dog. I could hear his inward groan from the car when I drove up.

He wanted me there (I hope) to give him a change of pace, and to give Mum a change of face, but I'm sure at times he also wished we would all just leave him alone.

Although our family had naturally dissipated and my brother and I had created our own families, it was right that my dad and my brother and I should come back together to care for my mum. We didn't just do it out of love but out of a duty to give back. Mum had slaved for us, sacrificed for us and, more often than not, she hadn't been appreciated or even thanked. So now, we gave her everything we could, because she deserved it. But slowly the need to care for my dad became as important as the need to care for my mum. In a way, Mum was cared for. We had all the practical decisions made. It was my dad whom we needed to watch. Every carer needs a carer. Caring for someone full-time is emotionally, physically and financially stressful. Carers are at a high risk of depression, unsurprisingly.

We had to make sure our primary carer had lots of respite and time away, and holidays when he was able to abdicate all responsibility.

This could lead to strange family assemblies. One year, my brother flew over to stay with Mum, my sister-in-law looked after their kids and my husband looked after ours, and I took Dad on a walking holiday to Majorca. When we got there, very unlike him, he wanted me to do all the driving, thinking and decision making. (I had a feeling he regretted this as he clung, white-knuckled, teeth-gritted to the passenger seat door as I negotiated bendy clifftop roads in the hire car.) Shifting from a lifetime of being the patriarch to allowing my brother and me to take charge of everything was a shock to us children. But keeping our focus on him became an important factor.

★ ★ ★

In 2013, we decided to do something special. My dad has climbed the Mourne Mountains all his life and has written several books about the area and so we decided to make a family trip. It required impressive logistical operations but we all played our part. My brother and his family flew over for the weekend and

I drove up with the girls from Dublin. Simon drove down to Newcastle where the base of the Mournes lie and met me with my girls. He took them off for a few hours and I had the privilege of climbing Slieve Donard with my dad on his eightieth hike to the summit. Just him and me on top of the world. When we had descended, my sister-in-law and my mum, who had travelled down in the Pat-mobile, met up with Dad and me, and Simon and the girls, and we all had a family picnic in Tollymore Forest Park at the base of the mountains, a place of our childhood, a place that meant so much to us all. It had been a risk. We didn't know if Mum could take an hour in the Pat-mobile, but she arrived in a good mood. When Dad and I descended from our climb, she smiled in love and recognition. Her family were all together again, in a magical place and, even though she had forgotten it by the next day, it is a memory that the rest of us can keep.

* * *

It was inevitable that we tried to push the limits. One of my biggest upsets when Mum had her stroke was that she would never come down to my house again. Never sit in the garden with me so we could feel the sun on our faces. I would never hear their car on the gravel or see her face light up in appreciation of my carefully rearranged cushions. As part of pushing the limits of Plan B, my brother was the one brave enough to suggest it. He decided it could be done, and therefore it would.

In the spring of 2013, he had arranged for a hired air-pressured bed and a hoist to be delivered to my house and found a carer in Dublin to come and help me. I would have to do all Mum's changes, washing and dressing, but I would have help. The big unknown was how Mum would cope with a two-and-a-half-hour drive from Belfast to Dublin so my brother flew over to sit in the Pat-mobile with Mum and Dad on the drive down.

I was so nervous. I had cleaned the house and made lots of food. The weather forecast for the whole four days was for torrential rain, but it didn't matter. We didn't have to go out, it was enough to have Mum here, in my home with the girls. I waited and waited and waited, and then I heard it. Their car on the gravel. I went to the front door and there she was. My mum, back at my house. And sitting on her knee was a Tupperware box full of goodies, this time made by my dad. His rocky roads have entered the Family Goodies Collection.

Despite the forecast, the sun hung high and bright in a cloudless sky, a little gift from life. As we pushed Mum into my sunlit kitchen, her face broke into a smile and she gasped, 'It's gorgeous.' We lifted her chair into the garden and, once again, we sat, smiling, holding hands, our faces turned to the sun.

It was hard work. Caring for Mum was back-breaking and physically difficult, but it was worth it. We did it. We had gotten her down to Dublin and my dad got a break and my mum got to see the girls come home from school and do their homework. My house is open plan so we were able to wheel Mum's bed into the kitchen or the lounge and she was included in everything we did.

It had been such a success, we decided to push it again.

I really do Christmas. I start about September and by December I'm in a state of glittered glory and Santa insanity. It had been devastating to me to think that Mum would never be in my home again at this time. Plan A was gone and the Christmases since Mum's stroke had been spent in their house, trying to make the best of it. But now we had decided we were going to kick the shit out of Plan B.

Christmas 2014, once again, I heard their car on my gravel on Christmas Eve, and my dad tumbled out laden down with presents and bottles and his homemade Christmas cake. My mum's face lit up when she saw my tree and said, 'It's so beautiful.' Plan B was never, ever, ever going to be as good as Plan A. But it was alright.

And then the cracks in Plan B began to appear.

★   ★   ★

For four years my mum had held on valiantly, mostly because my dad, Simon and I had no intention of letting her do anything else.

While my brother and I certainly did as much as we could, we were only the icing on top of a considerably dense structure. Dad's twenty-four-hour care of her was the cake that sustained her. I feel really blessed to have had the chance to witness the love which had been often unobserved as we grew up. Mum and dad had a tempestuous marriage, riddled with the usual pressures of life, and strife. (I could even have put a few 'verys' in there.) But as I was learning, when Mum had her stroke and they were stripped of the pressures and everyday minutiae of life, they were left with the base of their relationship, love.

For years, that love was sometimes hidden

by hostility and pressure, but when everything else is stripped away, love is all that is left. When the fight for rights, and values and the need to be heard was gone, my mum's face just shone with love for him. His was, and is still, the only name she can remember and say: 'David'. When the pressure to prove, and control, and the need to be heard was gone, my dad's face softened with love for her. But sometimes love can be hard, as we were about to find out.

It's a basic human reaction to save. Saving a life is instinctive, whereas waving a life goodbye feels like taking that bungee jump all those years ago — every inch of you resists it. Although the doctors and her family and her friends had saved Mum's life, she wasn't really living. She was merely existing in a half-life, with very little stimulation or joy or pleasure. Sure, we could put a smile on her face, but not for long.

On her eightieth birthday in 2014 we threw a garden party for her, and we dressed her up and did her hair and put her face on and she looked amazing, surrounded by all her family and friends. But then her will began to diminish. It was harder to engage her, harder to amuse her, harder to comfort her. She had been hospitalised twice for infections and pain and, each time, the trauma had taken a little more from her. And from us.

I had always thought adulthood began at eighteen. One thing that life has taught me is that there is still an awful lot of growing up to be done after that. Becoming an adult is more like a long stairway with many steps that begins much earlier and lasts much longer than a day on a calendar when you are handed your first legal drink.

I can still remember the first time I cried alone. I was a child of about ten, about Daisy's age now, standing on the darkened landing outside my bedroom door. I had been asleep, or perhaps couldn't sleep, and I was scared and wanted comfort. But something stopped me. I leaned over the landing banisters as the sounds of the TV filtered up. I don't know why I needed comfort or why I decided not to call down. I knew my mum would have been straight up to me. But I decided to face it alone. I cried out for my mum but not loud enough to be heard. I have often thought of that little girl — and wondered is that where I first learned my resilience? Is that where it began? Resilience I would have to lean on and build on time and time again in my life. And will my little girl start to cry and one night I won't hear her and, in doing so, will she realise that despite being so loved, she is in fact alone in a way that is empowering? And when she understands this, will she start to build herself? I know that resilience is one of the greatest gifts I can give my girls. That, and the knowledge that they are so loved, because they were the lessons I learned as a child.

As an adult, I had the love and support of so many people, but I was also alone now. I couldn't call my mum — she couldn't help me now. I did have lots and lots of friends to call, and they would and could comfort me. But sometimes you need to remind yourself of your own resilience. I needed to know my own resilience. To stand alone at the top of the stairs and cry and realise that perhaps I had the strength in me to manage.

I recently confessed to my eldest daughter that I was, in fact, the Tooth Fairy. She had looked at me dubiously. A sustained campaign of chocolate and gin do not a waif-like woman make. But I had fluttered my invisible wings and told her I believed in magic, and that life has an amazing way of delivering beauty and glitter, but that while I could never say for sure that fairies exist, I knew the Tooth Fairy did, because it was me. I said I had taken her teeth initially and left a treat as a way of making her feel safe through changes in her little life. I told her that while she grows up — through all the scary and exciting things that growing up entails — I would be by her side. My mum had stayed by my side long after I left home. Through all my growing up in my twenties and thirties, and becoming a mum myself, she still helped me up each step of the stairway of adulthood. And so, I told Daisy, I would always be by her side, as she goes through all the stages of growing up. It will take many forms, my support, and this form just happened to be a fairy.

My mum's support had taken many forms, and I knew I could cry alone because I always knew she would come if I called out loud enough.

I realised I hadn't become a real adult and I wouldn't take the final step on the stairway of adulthood until the day I knew Mum could no longer help. I was finally on the last step. It wasn't until I lost my mum that I finally became an adult.

Now my mum seemed to be ready to leave the stairway and let go of life. The magic she always kept in her eyes was dimming. The love was still there but it was tired. The smile still smiled, but not as wide. She was done crying alone, and she was done with being grown up. And that was OK. My role now was to finally step up and be the grown-up at the top of the stairs. And so as Mum let go, I reached out my hand and started to help my daughter with her first few shaky steps on the stairway. She has a long, long, long way to go, but as I told her that night, I will be by her side as long as I can.

I had reached the top step of the adult stairway and my grief no longer concerned what was best for me in having my mum live on. It was about what was best for her in letting her go. And I could come to that conclusion because after everything, feeling so many times like I knew nothing, I found that I knew something. When all else is stripped away, the only thing left is love. Love will always be there. And sometimes that has to be enough.

The gaping hole Mum's stroke created in our lives remained. I had just managed to put a wooden plank across it so I didn't fall in. But sometimes the plank moved. Even after several years, a lifetime of habit still haunted me. There were still moments when I forgot, and then relived the grief all over again. It could be something simple or something funny. Like the day I was pulled in to Ruby's Montessori to receive a complaint about her feisty nature in the same week her older sisters were given exemplary school reports. I thought it was funny, indicative of Ruby's gorgeous spirit. I was walking down the school corridor laughing to myself when I took out my phone and dialled Mum's number. I nearly threw up when a strange voice told me the number was no longer in service. Four years on, I had completely forgotten.

★ ★ ★

Being a part-time carer was challenging. I simply do not know how my dad did it full-time. Mum's confusion, the lack of conversation, the practical responsibilities and the emotional needs.

Occasionally, my dad had very reluctantly put Mum into a care home for very short periods of time to garner some respite and visit my brother or me, or go away alone. For everyone involved, it was a necessary evil. My mum always had a horror of old people's homes. I think they call them something different now — care homes, or residential homes for the elderly. They may have changed the name, but the smell is still the same. Dried, set in, there-to-stay-no-matter-how-much-the-place-is-cleaned urine and boiled vegetables. It probably stems from the years she had to watch her own mother, my Nanna Gypsy, shrivel and disappear into herself in one. My mum had lived through her own

Sandwich Years, caring for two small children and nursing her dad, and then her mum.

Her dad went quickly enough, his last cough bringing up a black slick of tar that dribbled down his chin. When my distraught mum asked the nurse what it was, she simply replied, 'It's his lung.' A smoking habit formed at the age of twelve had finally taken its toll on his ancient body.

But my nanna lingered, languishing in a geriatric hospital ward for months, and then in a care home for years, her mind lost long before her body caught up. I remember occasionally going to see her and her ghostly shadow frightened me. She had been a big-bosomed woman and here she was a little sparrow. She ranted and spoke no sense and my poor mum would hold her hand and try to be seen by those unseeing eyes, bearing the grief of knowing her own mother had forgotten who she was long ago.

We had considered putting Mum into a home in the weeks following her stroke. It was already traumatic that she was left to wear a nappy. The betrayal of putting her in one of 'those places' was unbearable. That Dad was able to care for her at our home with the help of a care package saved us from the guilt of putting Mum into a home, but the guilt then shifted to the thought that Dad had to carry the burden. The support my brother and I gave never felt like enough.

Dad has had a monitor in his bedroom since my mum was brought home, and every night the carers come in about 3 a.m. to change her. They make a noise and greet her loudly to make sure she is awake and they don't frighten her when they touch her. My dad has listened to this every night for the past five years. At least with a baby you know they will eventually sleep through the night. As a carer to an adult, disrupted sleep could, and does, go on indefinitely.

So it came to be that in order to give Dad respite to go on holiday, or come and see us in our homes, we did put Mum in care several times. My brother and I did a recce of all the local care homes, and it happened that the one we liked best was walking distance (or wheeling distance on a good day) from our family house.

It was lovely, as care homes go. The décor was faded. The smell was masked by Dettol and flowers so it wasn't an assault on the senses, even if it kind of whispered *death is around the corner*. The staff were amazing.

I'll never forget leaving Mum in for the first time, my voice bright with fake joy, her eyes brittle with real pain. She begged me not to leave. But I had to. I had come up to look after her for the first half of Dad's week away, but now I had to go back. I had three children waiting for me in Dublin and, once again, the choices and conflict demoralised me. I cried all the way down the motorway, guilty at the thought of her being there all on her own.

As I was leaving the care home, I passed a room where the hollow husk of a woman lay, crying out for someone who couldn't hear her. I wondered was my mum calling out for me, too. I'll never know, but her voice followed me all the way home anyway.

Over the years, we have all adjusted to those times. But no matter how wonderful the home was, or how amazing the staff were, it was dreadful leaving her there, her face like a betrayed child being abandoned in the woods. Always. As we now entered the fifth year of Mum's care we could see the toll it was taking on everyone, my dad especially. We knew we had to do something more.

★   ★   ★

It felt as though my mum was slowly coming to an end. She was losing interest in food, in the garden and even in us. Her body was healthy and alive but her spirit was weary. From the very first week in hospital, as she lay stricken by the stroke, her eyes had told me this was not what she wanted. Her eyes that had always told me so much, told me that. I distinctly remember wishing it would all end for her, there and then. I was delirious and sleep-deprived and in shock, but the thought, the urge, the need, was so acute, I can feel it still.

On the third day in hospital, I had sat beside her and laid my head on her pillow. I had whispered in her ear that I loved her, and that she had enriched my life. But in those few moments I really wanted her life to be over. I wanted her pain to be gone. I didn't want her to endure this. I wanted her to go with her dignity intact. But I wasn't strong enough to give up my need of her. As I lay there, my head next to hers, I was glad she was still alive.

Over the years, her eyes and eventually her words asked me repeatedly to make it all stop. 'I don't want this anymore,' she would say, her voice trembling.

We were all slowly coming to the conclusion that Plan B needed to be revised. We had had plans. We had had so much to do. That first night in the hospital I had screamed silently into the silence, 'This is not your day!' . . . but now, sometimes, I wished it had been. Because she had wished so much for her day to come, I now finally wished it too. To know that some day I would have to take my first breath in the moment after she has taken her last, in a world without my mum, still filled me with horror. But seeing her daily horror was worse.

To watch the woman you love in pain, to watch her die as her brain is slowly sapped through sheer lack of stimulation, the humiliation and degradation of nappies, and people wiping her and rolling her and wiping the shit from her bum and up her back, the spoon-feeding, the talking around, about and above her; hoisting her in a precarious crane, lying in her own shit and wee because the carers were not due for another hour. To see this was tragic. We thought we had been giving her the best care we could. But in doing so, had we given her the worst life possible?

My mum could live for years, but little by little she lived less. We wondered if, though, despite the fact that the stroke took every ability away from her, along with every decision and every choice, perhaps she was taking one last decision and making one last choice for herself. She was opting out because we didn't have the strength to do it for her. So we needed to move on from Plan B. That had been about helping her to live well. We had to think about Plan C, helping her to die well.

Increasingly, I began to ask the questions. Just because we can save a life, should we? Especially when that life is an insult to the life previously led. Have we reached a stage in modern medicine where advances are doing more harm than good? There is a very good chance that if Mum had had her stroke twenty years earlier she would have died. While there is lots of talk about ending lives through euthanasia, are we, as a society, really thinking through the many issues of prolonging lives? I really think there needs to be a greater dialogue about some sort of balance between longevity and quality of life. It seems all the medical advances in many conditions have made death, the most acute condition of all, more prolonged, emotionally painful and complicated.

When health deteriorates to a point where life is made unbearable, should we keep prolonging it just because we can? In an attempt to over-care, are we over-treating?

I have no regrets about what we did for my mum. We had said all we had to say, we had done all we could have done. I now wanted her to have peace.

When she first had her stroke I hadn't been prepared for her death. Now I think I was.

When she first had her stroke I desperately wanted her to live. Now I didn't. When she first had her stroke I hadn't been able to contemplate a world without her. I still couldn't, but I was finding it increasingly difficult to live in a world where my mum lived such a life. The life she had lived was over. The life she lived now needed to be over. It had taken me four years to come to terms with that. Four years of grief and desperation. The grief will always be with me, but the desperation had changed. I realised I had to make a grown-up decision.

Plan B had dictated that when Mum was sick, we immediately tried to save her. We called an ambulance and had her admitted to hospital. Being bed-bound in a bed that was too big to go through the door meant that Mum had to be lifted by several people holding the corners of her sheet, and carried through the doorway into the hall where the ambulance gurney waited. This caused her an enormous amount of distress. Then she would be put on a ward with poor people who looked like extras from Michael Jackson's 'Thriller' video, and inevitably tubes would be inserted by strangers (lovely nurses, but not the carers she was used to). Old age knows no limits to indignity.

Because her official name is Mary Patricia,

her admission document always gave this name. So the staff called her Mary even though she is called Pat. They would call her the wrong name and give her tea the wrong way (she takes it black, and tea on the stroke ward is always served white). It's the little things. But they are enormous when you are alone and frightened and half your brain is damaged and you cannot move or get away and you can't speak the thoughts that are in your head and ask for help. They call you the wrong name, and they give you tea you don't like, and you can't ask for help. And they take you for tests and scans and give you injections and pills, and it is a frightening, traumatic experience.

I felt the tension in me every time I visited her in hospital, my mum lying like a frightened bird, while I got a black marker from the nurses' station to write as big as I could on the whiteboard behind her bed 'PAT' and then in smaller writing, 'Black Tea'. Her dignity was reduced to a white-board message that went mostly unseen.

Into our fifth year, my mum was still hanging on. We all were. My dad, my brother, me. All getting a little more tired, a little older, a little less able.

She didn't want to live, because she knew she wasn't living. She became so low and her distress was unbearable to watch. For a time she had stopped allowing us to get her up into her chair. One of the only things that had made any of this manageable was the fact we could hoist her into a wheelchair and get her up most days for a couple of hours. But no more. Not moving for years had taken its toll. She had pain in her legs. But really she had pain in her heart. We all did. To watch the woman you love more than any other endure a life like this was crushing. To live it must have been like being buried alive. Buried under the rubble of the life you'd had.

When Dad called me to say she was sick because the pain-relief medicine the GP had given her had made her too drowsy and now she was dangerously dehydrated, I immediately said, 'Call the ambulance.' But as soon as I put down the phone I felt as I had done in that hospital room at the very beginning when I laid my head on her pillow, unable to stop this nightmare for her. I felt like I had failed her again.

Had my mum died in the first week, the shock would have nearly killed me. All that love and all those plans, gone in an instant with no chance to say goodbye or hold her hand or come to terms with it. The fear of her dying was a crippling physical presence, like a disease inside me. Every morning, I woke up and pulled back the curtains and searched the sky. *Is this the day she will die?* I'd wonder, terrorised by the fear that it would be. But as the curtain went back day by day, I stopped searching the sky, now terrorised by the fear that this could go on and on, slowly diminishing her until there was nothing left in her world.

For several years we were able to manage things OK. Plan B was working. We had saved her life, and, in doing, so I had saved my own. This time with her had given me a chance to adjust, to grieve, to be practical and care for her, to hold her hand and paint her nails, to believe I was still making her life better. But what price did she pay?

As we began our fifth year, what started out as a slow, painful murmuring for my dad, brother and me to each get to the same point where we all knew that this couldn't go on, finally escalated to a definite consensus. We decided that after several bouts of emergency hospital admissions, we had to look into a Plan C. Not to wouldn't have been fair to her.

While Mum was in hospital this time, my wonderful sister-in-law Charlotte, who is also a doctor, arranged for her to be seen by a geriatrician as a whole person under his care, rather than carrying on with the several doctors seeing her for different bits of her like her stroke, depression or UTIs. And we made a plan that would mean less intervention. Less emergency response. Less saving, and more making comfortable.

And this is where we are now. Living Plan B, knowing if we need it, we have a Plan C, and hoping that we all have the strength to stick with it when the call comes. I know we are right, but I hope I keep my nerve when Dad calls to say she is sick, and that I'm not standing in Tesco with three children and, instead of saying in my instinctive Save Voice, 'Call the ambulance', I have the strength and the love to say in my Heartbroken Brave Voice, 'OK, call the geriatrician. Call the palliative care team. Let's keep her at home, and make her comfortable.' I hope we all do, before we abandon our lives to be with her while she finally abandons hers.

I have found many voices as I have grown up as a strong independent woman, but this is the voice I needed to find most. I hope when the time comes, I can.

10

Perfection Is for Perfectionists

Our Plan C had been agreed with heavy hearts. But, around this time, as Mum was in hospital and as we rallied around her and Dad, I was hit by another blow. My marriage ended at the same time as my mum had started to deteriorate.

It happened suddenly, throwing me into another, though very different, emotional tailspin.

While we agreed a new plan for Mum, I agreed away my marriage.

Separation is just another form of limbo grief. No matter why a relationship ends, it is final curtains on a dream you once had and a future you thought was yours. And like losing a parent, or having a miscarriage, the end of a marriage is depressingly common.

Yet for every family and every individual, it is a catastrophic experience. I had become yet another statistic. I was beginning to hate statistics.

Like other forms of grief, separation has stages and processes dressed up in different hats — shock, loss, anger, shock, loss, powerlessness, loss, murderous anger, fear — but, at the end of the day, underneath each hat was simply just grief. No matter which hat that grief wore each day, it always came with its twin brother, pain.

Like any loss, the pain is extraordinary. Breathtakingly sleep-suckingly, ground-shakingly extraordinary. And, like grief, it's not just the feeling you have to contend with, which you can mask sometimes with the everyday routine of life and a lovely glass of gin. There is the practical slicing up of a life, the dissection and laceration of a body of time, until all you are left with are the entrails of a relationship and a bloody and bruised heart.

We went to mediation to work out how to separate logistically. This dealt with practical stuff, like money and our children. There is no mediation for the emotional stuff, like grief and hatred, loss and love.

Eventually though, we finalised the six-page document which now represented my husband in absence. It was full of rules and drop-off times and weekend shifts and divided school holidays. It was full of numbers and figures and how much I could spend a month on tampons. Literally. There was a line for hair, and a line for food, and a line for pet insurance and a line for going out.

There was no line for love.

It was full of facts and empty of emotion. I used to have a marriage. Now I had a spreadsheet. I used to have hugs. Now I had maintenance. I used to have love. Now I had rules. I was taking a battering.

There are the days when you have the strength to deflect the little blows life throws at you. Like a martial arts expert, a hand shield here, a step back there. Deflect, desist, defend. Then there are times when all you can do is stand there and let life slap you around the face with a wet fish. You just have to live through the pain. Absorb it into yourself and cry, and know you will come out the other side. When the framework that holds your life together — a marriage under which you sacrifice, have children, compromise — is suddenly taken away, you are left with nothing but wobbly sides.

I was left a single parent at the same time my mum had started to deteriorate and we had to look at Plan C. And, once again, the acuteness of my Sandwich Years lacerated me. My girls needed me most when my mum needed me most — their world was shattering and my mum's was drifting and I was caught in the snowstorm of shrapnel. Mum was increasingly distressed. She had had enough. I was distressed. I was enduring enough. My children were distressed. Their family was now never going to be enough. Oh George Clooney where were you?

Mum became ill again and I had to leave my girls once more to be up with her, knowing I should also be there for them. She cried, she clasped my hand and begged me to make it all stop. She wanted it all to stop. She needed me to just hold her and be there, and I'm so glad I was there. But by being there I wasn't with the other people who needed me . . . my girls.

My daughters would call me, unable to speak with the hysteria of hurt. They were enduring the breakup of their family, their foundation, their life as they knew it. Sometimes, they would weep down the phone, begging me to come home, my heart splintering into shards that I couldn't be there for them. It wasn't that they didn't want to be with their dad. They just didn't want that to mean they couldn't be with me.

So, once again, I was pulled apart — my mum and my daughters, both pleading and needing, both in despair. And I was caught in their anguish, trying to fix the unfixable. I needed my mum to help me through and it made me miss her all over again.

* * *

It might be hard parenting without a parent to help out. It's even harder parenting without a partner to help out. He is a good, devoted dad but he now had his days to parent and I had mine. I was feeling like a limp sandwich filled with life's off-meat. Squashed between caring for a now-disintegrating young family and a now-struggling elderly family, I felt my job was somehow to be the lick of jam that made their lives sweet and tasty.

I have had to leave my children over and over again, and the wrench this caused has left a neediness in us all when we are together. It's not that I'm a Helicopter Mum, more of a Mini Cooper Mum, driving madly behind them wherever they went. At least I was leaving the children with the other half of the parenting partnership.

When our marriage ended, I was faced with them being taken away from me regularly. While I had to come to terms with what I was losing, I had to also get to grips with what he was taking. Most of the week and the weekends I had them, I parented alone. The weekends he had them, I sat alone or went to Belfast. The added pressure of my domestic workload was intense. I was afraid I might fall apart. I needed my mum more than ever, but she couldn't even say my name. She knew nothing of my pain, because what was the point of making her life any worse than it already was? My dad and I had almost come to blows on this matter the first weekend I went up after the split. They had loved my husband like a son, and my dad didn't want my mum upset.

'You cannot tell your mum,' he told me. But all I wanted to do was crawl under the duvet with her and be her child and feel her love and have her make me feel OK. I was really upset, but he was resolute.

'You only want to tell her to make yourself feel better. That's selfish.'

I hated him that weekend, but he was right. I had reached the top step of adulthood and I was teetering on a very thin piece of ground. So I smiled and scraped the dirt out of her nails, washed her teeth and cleaned their house and wished more than anything my old mum could come back and hold me like she used to, and make me a cup of tea and for a few moments, make everything feel OK.

I sat holding her hand, my heart bleeding for my girls whose hands I couldn't hold because they were now on 'Daddy time'.

The sharpness of my Sandwich Years cut deep once again. The pressures were stretching me thin. I had to put my children first this time and that meant not being as supportive to Mum and Dad as I wanted to be. I was back to making critical choices. I was standing in a world of question marks, trying to take care of everyone and figure out where the answers were. But I had to acknowledge that the pressures I put on myself didn't help.

★   ★   ★

I've reached the top of the stairway to adulthood, and it's a responsible place. And the most important thing I've learned on my journey up that stairway is that I can't do it all.

Mum and I had always spent a lot of time together, but that's not to say we didn't argue. We argued a lot, about nothing and everything. I sometimes didn't have time for her. Because sometimes the love I felt for my mum was overwhelmed by the annoyance. My first instinct on many an occasion over the years had been to tut as soon as the phone rang, because I knew it would be her. For all my mum's goodness and love, she also irritated the hell out of me at times. No shock there. I think it's safe to say that while (on the whole) no-one will ever love you like your mum, no-one can quite push your buttons like your mum either. This is probably because they set the nuclear codes. They embed the secret detonation programme in our DNA during pregnancy, the red button under a code pad that only they have the key to. (Or was that just me?) It can be something as innocent as a throwaway comment (but are they ever throwaway, or are they always loaded with hidden dynamite, a ticking time bomb designed to blow up in your face, an 'Are you really wearing that?').

Take a tuna sandwich. I remember one lunchtime when Daisy and Poppy were very small, my mum came to stay, and she took half an hour to make a tuna sandwich. Half an hour! I was incandescent. In the time it took her to butter two slices of bread, open a tin, spread some mayo and slam it all together (although in fairness, she would never slam, but gently place together — herein lay the beginnings of our differences), I had fed Poppy, detached a screaming Daisy from her self-imposed prison under the dining room chair, prepared our dinner, read half the paper, watched the news headlines, put the babes to bed and sent two text messages. I was about to start hoovering the house in a fit of agitated pique when the plate finally arrived in front of me. It certainly looked the same as mine would have. It didn't seem to taste any different from the ones I make. But there it was in all its glory — the Half Hour Tuna Delight.

And so began one of those mother-daughter debates. She said I did everything too fast — I ate too fast, I talked too fast, I walked too fast, I drove too fast. Of course, I spluttered my indignation at such suggestions — didn't she understand I had so much to do? If I didn't do everything at warp speed, I'd fail as a mother, and the house would disintegrate around our very ears and I'd never get anything done. As for the children, how else was I supposed to get through the day if I didn't move at Olympic pace? She gave me that look. The look that says, *Oh please. You think you have it hard now? Try doing all that but with none of the time-saving devices you have — I had no proper washing machine, no tumble dryer, no microwave oven, no steriliser, no disposable nappies, no car! And by the way, how did I produce such a drama queen?*

It's amazing how much one's mother can say with one slightly raised eyebrow. Naturally I pooh-poohed her with that condescending tone that we reserve for our mothers, something along the lines of, 'In your day, you didn't have half the pressures we modern mums do,' and raced off to hang the washing out in one minute flat. But I know she was right.

I'd barely finished one task before my mind had moved on to the next. My children must have wondered who the mad woman was who attacked them with a facecloth every morning before ramming a toothbrush into their mouths, swirling it around and yakking at them to 'Spit!' before they'd swallowed their last bite of breakfast. I'm not sure I'd ever actually walked down my front path to the car — I'm usually just a blur of movement dragging one child by the arm with fourteen bags hanging off the other, shouting at the older ones to hurry up.

But now I wish more than anything I had taken time while she made that tuna sandwich, and instead of being incandescent with rage, that I had simply sat on the stool and listened to her talk.

Sometimes I move so fast I see myself rushing past in a blur of colour. 'Oh is that me?' I think as I whip past. But before I can grab myself, I'm gone, like a gust of wind, the only sign left of me a rustle of the trees and the dog spinning in my jet stream. Sometimes I watch him in the garden chasing his tail and I think, 'Yep, that's me,' without the drool.

My mum always told me I suited hats. I just never imagined how many I'd have to wear. Life was so simple in my twenties. I was just me. I wasn't fully sure who 'me' was, but that was all I had to figure out. That, and which boy to kiss. But life became more complex with every year and now, between parenting, daughtering, working, writing, separating and socialising, I have so many hats that my scalp is itching and my eyes are twitching. And I feel half mad.

On a good day, I get to take one hat off before I put on another, and hopefully have a nice cup of tea in between. But that is rare. Most days, I have to jump and juggle in a peculiar pantomime — keeping all my hats in the air and swapping them around at high speed. Put one on, whip it off, put another on, pull it off, put a different one on, zip it off, put the other one back on, quick, quick — some days I tell the dog to set the table and call one of my clients 'sweetheart' on the phone. Once, I threw the phone for the dog and kept talking to the plastic bone. The phone bone squeaked and he chewed the bone phone.

Evenings are a mix of hats as I get work and chores done in between three bedtime routines. Sometimes, I feel like one of those silly clowns — a pile of hats stacked on my head as I play all hats together. I had spent the previous four years building up my sandwich filling from a tasteless, limp petrol station pre-wrap to a more identifiable, tasty delight that even had a thin layer of relish. But once again, my Sandwich Years reduced me to two crackers with a piece of out-of-date cheese in the middle. Life had brewed me up another perfect storm of need, and by this stage, I was so knackered I didn't even care that George Clooney hadn't made an appearance. (Typically, just as I became single, George went and got married. Sigh.) And I understand that if I don't slow down, then life might just do it for me.

Feminism has been great for allowing us to believe we can 'have it all'. But what that has meant for many of us is that we end up just 'doing it all'. Too much, too fast, under too much pressure. We keep going despite feeling tearful and fearful of the sheer volume of stuff we have to achieve.

The Wonder Woman pants I had worn for years had begun to give me a wedgie.

Many women have a tendency to strive for perfection, keep the boat afloat, even if that means paddling like a maniac. But research is showing that setting ourselves too high standards, and taking on too much, causes not only psychological stress but physical harm. We're not just losing our minds, we're losing our health.

It is estimated that two in five of us display perfectionist tendencies. Add on to that the number who just try and juggle too many balls and it's a wonder any of us are sane at all. We do it to each other. Anyone who trawls through Facebook or Twitter at night will see a slideshow of happy faces and happy families and happy happiness, which, when you're reaching for the gin because you've had another epic day of stress, can tip you over the edge. I'm guilty. I only ever post on a good day. On bad days, I go to ground. How come we never post those woke-up-with-a-spot-and-roots-showing-bags-under-eyes pictures, just the ones with good lighting and lift? Partly for me, I'm usually so tired on bad days, I don't even open my Facebook, and other times I'm just feeling too sorry for myself.

Research has found that socially prescribed perfectionists — those who believe other people like our parents, children, bosses and colleagues demand perfection from us — have declining physical health, make more visits to the doctor and take more sick days. (Hands up, this is me.) We rarely ask for help, or admit we are failing (or falling). We put ourselves under constant pressure to perform and it has unhealthy consequences.

Other sobering research shows that four in ten women in the UK feel 'on the brink of burnout', and there's nothing to suggest it isn't the same in Ireland.[7] 'Stress' used to be an illness. Now it's a way of life, a term as common as 'I'm tired' or 'I'm hungry'. Most of us accept that modern life, with all its amenities, also comes with modern strain. When we compare ourselves to the seemingly 'together' women around us, we will never measure up. What worries me — and I am as guilty as the next under-that-nicely-dyed-hair-is-a-grey-haired-woman — is our belief that we must. That we must keep running on empty long after our tank has run out of fuel. My mum may have made the perfect tuna sandwich, but she made sure to sit down and eat it slowly, sacrificing other bids for perfection for that moment. We are trying to forge ahead, often to manage a job, career, children, elderly parents, and hold it all together, whilst looking and being absolutely perfect. I'm done with perfect. I've thrown it out with my marriage. That doesn't mean I'm dropping all standards but the odd packet of bought biscuits or a TV dinner isn't going to kill my family. It might even save us.

Sometimes in life, it is so easy to keep running. It is so easy to put our heads down and go fast. But one thing my mum has taught me is to slow down.

I think we have so much to thank the

feminist sisters who came before us for. I think it's vital that we learn to 'lean in' as Sheryl Sandberg encourages. But I also think we need to be careful about the practical implications. I think it is imperative that we learn to lean back too, and have the mental equivalent of a cup of tea and a little bit of something nice. It's amazing what has been achieved and it's so important that we all reach for it, but on the whole, no-one has come along and taken away any of the other responsibilities — we still care for our kids, our parents, our partners; we have homes, and careers, or hybrid jobs, but in the midst of this we must try to have nourishment for ourselves. We have to allow ourselves to acknowledge that it's really hard.

LIFE IS REALLY HARD SOMETIMES!

While fighting for our space and our place in society, we also have to accept what is, and make the best of it. Perfection should only refer to a chocolate cake. It should not refer to ourselves. Instead of constantly wishing we could do better, we need to accept we do pretty damn good. Instead of constantly wishing we could do more, we need to accept we do enough — and make sure we are doing the *right* things, not *all* of the things.

There is a lot of terrible advice handed out to parents these days. But the one that I actually take note of now is the one they give out on a plane. 'Those with children please put on their own oxygen mask first.' If there is one thing these Sandwich Years have taught me it is that every carer (and every mother is a carer) needs a carer. And, sometimes, that carer needs to be you.

Our feminist forbears fought for a game-changing future for women. And while we need to continue to fight — for equal pay, for equality in the home, for protection from violence and threat, to be heard, to be seen, to be given the credibility we deserve — we also need to fight to be kind to ourselves. To focus on our potential to give it all, not have it all.

By the nature of our biology, we are the carers — we need to fight to make sure that we can also take care of ourselves. It is my experience of the Sandwich Years and, generally life that as we parent-care alongside childcare, we must also learn to self-care.

Burnout is a consequence of an increasingly frantic or bursting life and high expectations. Just because we *can* do it all, *should* we do it all? The problem with perfectionism is that it's not a side effect of feminism (although the modern media does

267

not help). Most of us impose it on ourselves.

As I have mentioned, I like order and planning. I immediately liked the concept of Montessori because every item has a place with its shape in an outline, so that children know where to put everything back. I like that, a dotted line to show me where everything in life goes. With everything that had happened since my mum's stroke, it felt at times as if all the lines had been rubbed out. I didn't know where everything should go. I felt I was standing in a storm and all my possessions were blowing about in the wind, and I was left to grab at whatever I could. There was so much loss and grief around me, but I had three children who needed care and comfort and so I put my face on every day. Just like I'd been taught.

After my marriage ended, I tried to manage my own grief, alongside that of my children, as well as keep them and the house afloat, and my job and support to Mum and Dad. People kept telling me I was strong. I would get through it. I'd be OK. I know they meant well and I know they meant it as a compliment, but somehow it made me flinch. It felt like they didn't understand my pain. Like they didn't understand that I put my face on because I had no choice. It reminded me of when I was a child and my mum would say, 'I never have to worry about you . . . I do worry about your brother though.' That hurt. My childish self would shout back silently, *But I want you to worry about me!* So now, when my gorgeous friends and those around me said, 'But Alana, you are so strong, you will come through this,' my little inner child pouted once more and shouted, *But I'm hurting!*

People kept telling me I was strong, and it upset me. I didn't feel strong. I felt rejected and bruised and not good enough. I felt a failure. I felt stressed and wrung out. At night, as I lay in bed, heart pounding, I was a gibbering wreck. I wasn't strong! I lay awake, calming my frantic heart. I ranted and raged and cried and wept and shouted at my children, because my inner child was never far away. It took going to my nourishing place, Donegal, to make me realise that often my strength came from the expectation others had of me, including myself. *Especially* myself. And that expectation was at a high I could not reach. If I was left to my own devices (if I could shut down that tiresome voice in my head that constantly tells me to be perfect), I'd just go and get a drive-thru KFC still dressed in my pyjamas and take it back to bed and watch a boxset of *Nashville*, back to back, licking my fingers and licking my wounds. Instead, I got up and took off the pyjamas and put my face on. Because it's not about strength, it's about survival. And it's something we are all programmed to do.

I used to pride myself on perfection (in my head at least). I liked to think of myself as a perfectionist, even though my mum would disagree. She actually *was* a perfectionist, and could sew and knit to professional standards while my knitting looks like a ball of wool after the kitten has played with it, and the cushions I sewed are currently spewing threads and filling all over my sofa. But back in my head, I'm a perfectionist. No point in doing anything if it isn't going to be done *now*, and done well.

I exhaust some of my friends with my quick turn-around from decision to delivery . . . within three weeks of my marriage ending, I had redecorated my bedroom, complete with vintage furniture from eBay and my long-longed-for hummingbird-print wallpaper. I hasten to add that in hindsight, I think that was the only way I could take charge of a situation that was spiralling out of control — I could do practical because there was no way I was able to do emotional.

So perfectionism has driven me most of my life — to very good effect. But it has also damaged me.

Escaping to Donegal again last summer, sitting by the sea one day I had a sea change.

Something about that sky makes me realise how far my horizons can go. Something about that solitude makes me hear my own voice. Something about that beauty makes me see a better view of my life. I sat on the beach, my girls swimming and kayaking in the water, having the real swallows and amazons holiday they need every year, where everything is just stripped away until only themselves and nature are left — and I had a revelation.

In the turmoil of separating, I had been constantly sick with one or other awful thing (abscesses, chest infections, cold sores and migraines to name but a few). I had been stressed, I had been agitated and whiney with the girls at times; I had been angry, I had been hurt, I had been overwhelmed, I had been soul-sad and will-weary. And as if that wasn't all bad enough, I decided to heap a big dollop of guilt like a big red cherry on top of the melting ice-cream sundae of my life.

I was actually annoyed at myself for all of those things, for not being perfect.

I had set myself a standard whereby I could sail through the worst time of my life, all smiles and strength, and I was failing miserably. But survival is not the same as strength and, for most of the Sandwich Years,

I was not strong. I merely survived. But, somehow, through surviving, I had gained strength.

I realised that being strong is what I am. It is who I am. And I am finally proud of it. I was strong, and yes, I was hurting. But I was not hard. I was loving and that is what made me strong. And that is what this life took from me for a while. The belief in my loving strength. And that is what I am reclaiming. I am strong and I love and protect the people around me, even when I'm hurting.

I often felt bruised by life's slapping during those months, and as I sat in the quiet of my house, my marriage reduced to a six-page document, I wondered how I would pick myself up. Eventually I did what I often did — I thought of my mum.

She'd had a hard life at times, but she'd endured it with love and kindness. No matter how crap it had become, she'd say she was off to put her face on, which also meant her strength to carry on, her love and kindness.

Recently, Daisy stood in front of my bedroom mirror and preened herself with my makeup brushes. 'I'm just going to put my face on!' she said in her best mummy voice. The chain chinks as Mum's voice reaches her through me. And it made me smile. My girls learn from me, as I learned from my mum. It's not about being false or being something you're not. It's about facing up to the bad times, facing down the challenging times and facing into the sun in the good times.

Life was hard back then. But I was determined to face up to it, face it down and wait for a time when I was facing into the sun. And when you can't stand around waiting for the sun to shine, you just have to learn to dance in the rain.

As I sat on the beach that day in Donegal, I decided to put my Wonder Woman pants in the wash and accept that, for now, my life was not perfect, and so I wasn't going to kill myself making myself perfect either. And to remember that, like Donegal in the rain, my life was still pretty spectacular. I had three amazing girls, a heritage of love from my family, wonderful friends who reminded me that I didn't need to be perfect and loved me for *me*, a business doing something I loved, and most of all, like the Donegal sky, a limitless horizon.

After we returned home, I realised I had to make some decisions for the sake of my mental health — and therefore the sake of my family. I buried the Wonder Woman aspiration. I cremated the Yummy Mummy goal. I sucked the spotless house ambition up the hoover. I prioritised. I took breaks. I even broke my cardinal rule of no telly during the day, and sometimes let the girls watch it while I went back to bed with a cup of tea and my book. And the parenting police didn't come and lock me up.

I've spent years waiting for my life to be perfect. Waiting for a time when I can get enough sleep, a time when there are no dramas, a time when there is no hassle and the computer always works, a time when there is no stress. I'm done waiting. This is life. It is hectic and busy and frantic and full of love and full of heartache, and it has good days and bad days, boredom and loneliness, happiness and laughter, stress and strife, fun and family. It has days when I don't get time to go to the loo, and days when the girls and I just stay in our pyjamas. It is the life that I have, and it is perfectly good for me.

My life is not perfect. But it doesn't need to be. And neither do I.

11

Surviving and Thriving

The years of caring for children, or parents, or building our careers can make for a rocky road. They can be full of pain and grief, and relentless choices and hard work. But they can also be full of love, and learning and unity and growth. I look back on my earlier life and laugh at how innocent and carefree it was. Typical. You spend 35 years with no responsibility other than your job, and then like a number 15A bus, they all come at once: children, elderly parents, divorce and a proper grown-up job. Increasingly driven by us giving life later and parents holding onto life longer, more and more women are caught in that perfect storm of need and care. And there is no George Clooney.

In whatever manner they arrive, the Sandwich Years bring challenges few of us are prepared for. There is the grief that the person who has anchored your life is casting you adrift. There is the shock and fear of role-reversal, and the realisation you have reached the top step of adulthood. There are the practical, financial and emotional responsibilities of caring for your loved ones, which you had no idea you would or could face. There is the toll on your mental health as you struggle to juggle the needs of all those around you, often at the expense of your own. There is the loss of your identity, covered by layers and layers of hats that you wear as a mother, partner, daughter, colleague, friend, career person, until you realise that there is no hat left with just your name on it. There is the unsteady walk along the balance bar, with work and home and life tipping you every which way. There are awful decisions to be made about care, life and death. But. There is also the love you have and share with the people for whom you care. There are friends and family, and help, and gasmasks. There is rebooting and rebuilding and realising that you are not alone. Most of all, there is your own resilience. Your own strength. And hopefully, your own kindness to yourself. When we care for others, self-care is the most important care of all.

★ ★ ★

I was living in London when my mum turned 60. It was after university when my life was rich in new experiences and poor in cash, high-octane in social life and low-grade in paying jobs. How ancient I thought Mum was as I grasped life's hand, a wrinkle-free 24-year-old. I had left home and was embarking on an independent life. I loved it. I lived in many rooms, in many countries, and it would be a long time before I had my own space to call my place. But no matter where I went, no matter which country, or what room I resided in, my mum came with me. Metaphorically speaking, of course. Although I had detached from her physically, we always stayed connected, with letters, calls and visits. So I wanted to do something special for her sixtieth and decided to make her a book of her life. I bought a red leather book with black card pages and used beautiful silver and gold liquid pens to write notes and remarks with the photos I stuck in. It took me weeks as I contacted my family and her friends for thoughts and photos and Dad found me stuff from their attic — pictures of her as a girl, her first programme for a piano recital, references from her first jobs, pictures of all the houses they lived in, snapshots of memories, and a lifetime of experiences.

Seeing Mum as a young glamorous woman, on her wedding and then during the introduction of her new family, with her friends always a part of that, made me view her slightly differently, as a woman in her own right. On the last page was a picture of the four of us — Mum, Dad, Simon and me, grown up but still family. It was taken on a Christmas Day, and we are all laughing rather manically because Dad couldn't work out the camera timer, so it had taken longer to take the photo than cook the turkey, by which time much wine had been drunk and we were all slightly hysterical. It was a good place to end this Book of Life. I promised Mum that the remaining blank pages were for the next ten years, and then the next, and that I would update it every decade for her. In those days we all believed in our invincibility. Like most of us I'm sure, I believed I would still be doing it when my mum was 100 and I was turning 60 myself. She loved the book, and we would often sit and go through it, reminiscing. Her past and our past were always entwined in our present. It provided a tangible testimony to the chain we were part of, separate glittering circles of gold, but linked through new and old.

For Mum's seventieth though, I forgot to update her book. The previous ten years had been busy. I had worked and built up skills, gone travelling, begun a proper career, and finally met the man who would become my husband. We were too busy enjoying life, so I never quite got round to updating the book. Instead, for her birthday we all went on that gorgeous family holiday to Tuscany. Our family had expanded by then, and so my sister-in-law and little niece were there, and my husband-to-be, a new engagement ring glittering on my hand, our future glittering in front of us. Then, over the next half-decade, there were enough events to fill an entire new book — twin nephews, my wedding, holidays, Christmases, the birth of my two girls — events my mum was as much a part of as her smile in every photo. Then my Sandwich Years began and for the last few years of that decade, life went on for the rest of us but halted for her. For her eightieth birthday, I decided it was time to update her Book of Life. There wasn't the same joy in putting together the photos — some made me smile, but many of them hurt, especially the ones without her in them. But she was still there in many of them: the photo of her in Tollymore Forest Park after Dad and I had climbed the mountain, surrounded by the beautiful trees and her husband, her children and her grandchildren. There was the photo of her in my house in Dublin, sitting in my back garden, our faces turned to the sun. Photos of Christmas, of grandchildren on her knee or sitting on her bed, of lunches out with her friends, her lopsided smile showing love for us all still.

The final photo I put in her book was from her eightieth birthday party. There she was, dressed up and done up, sitting in her chair in a sunny, resplendent garden, surrounded by everyone who loved her. I thought about what we might have done in Plan A. A family holiday away somewhere, or perhaps a party like this where she would have blushed with the attention, but also worn herself out with lists and cooking. We all wished it could have been Plan A, but we were making the very best of Plan B for as long as it worked. The book of *her* life is a book filled with family and friends. Most of all, it is filled with the only thing that will be left when everything else is stripped away and when she herself is finally gone. Love. When the time comes, I will take it back and keep it on my shelf and remember how important her life was to so many of us. Until then, although we have Plan C in place, we will continue to make the best out of Plan B for as long as she needs us to, holding hands, and making memories still.

*　*　*

We often talk about being a parent as an endurance test, but being a daughter is an endurance test too. I sometimes saw myself as being pulled — my children on one side, my mum on the other — but increasingly I have come to see this relationship as a chain with no beginning or end. When I had Daisy, I became her world. When Poppy came along, I became her world and she wouldn't let me out of her sight for two years. But slowly something changed. They became friends, sitting side by side in their double buggy like peas in a pod. Still, for a long time, they were little selfish beings who just wanted me or Daddy. But as Ruby entered the fold I witnessed an extraordinary thing. Alongside the wonderful connection I have with each of my children, I watched how they developed unbreakable relationships with each other. I could step back a little now and watch from the sidelines as they fought, bickered, hugged, loved, laughed, joked, teased, encouraged, taught and learned from each other. I was still their world, but their universe was expanding so that we were all satellites, spinning around each other, giving and getting life. As my brother and I navigated the emotional, sometimes traumatic landscape of caring for our parents, I felt proud that our life together had stood us in good stead as we supported each other. (We annoyed each other too! As a child he once glued the last pages of my latest Famous Five book together so I couldn't read the ending. Brothers are very annoying. It comes in the job description.) But he has been a constant strength in my life, and like my dad, he always has my back. And so I can see that the beginnings of a lifetime of connections are forming now, ones that will help carry my daughters all through their life. And mine too. A chain of links, separate but always connected.

Just as I often open my mouth to speak and my mum comes out, so it has begun that my girls voice me. I will never forget the first time I saw Daisy act out an imaginary scene. I watched as she played with her doll, entranced by my baby's transformation into a little girl. My enchantment was short-lived when I realised Dolly was firmly placed on the naughty step and being boldly admonished by her 'Mummy'. I was absolutely gutted! All my loving, attention-giving, teaching and singing, all my playing and reading — and the one thing she copies is me being horrible! Thankfully though, as time went on, and especially after I had Poppy, Daisy acted out lots of the good 'Mummy' stuff too. I thought all my stitches would come out after Poppy was born when she tried to breastfeed her Dolly. Now, often the tables are turned when they use their

'Mummy' voice on me. 'What do you say?' they ask me with a superior but very sweet raised eyebrow if I give a hurried command while forgetting my manners. 'Please,' I say sheepishly. Ah yes, it was all coming back to haunt me. They make me laugh, taking charge of the world, in order to make sense of their own. We are all part of the same chain. I still have a set of Russian dolls I was given as a child. And sometimes that's how I feel about my relationship with Mum and my girls. Sometimes we stand alone, and sometimes we all fit inside each other.

My bracelet still jingles with the charms of my life. One for each of my daughters, and four little butterflies for the ones I also had the pleasure of loving, even for a little while. A star fish to remind me of my travels and the world at my feet. A little silver clam with a pearl inside given to me by my colleagues when I left work to remind me that the world is my oyster. I replaced the one that represented my marriage with a silver hive dotted with beautiful gold bees to remind me that my life is busy but sweet and full, and inscribed on the bottom are the words 'Be happy.' Finally I have the silver heart with my mum's handprint on it, forever guiding and holding my hand. As I have survived and finally begun to thrive through the Sandwich

Years, I have realised that her handprint isn't just hanging from the bracelet on my wrist. It is branded on my back, gently pushing me onward. And as I gently push my girls onward (whilst trying very hard not to grip the back of their T-shirts and haul them back), I know that what my mum taught me, I want to teach them. I want to teach my girls that it's the family we create as much as the family we have that will care for us. That feminism is as much about reaching out and asking for help — taking strength from the circle of sisters around us — as it is about standing up and being strong.

That life is not about 'having it all' (and certainly not 'doing it all') but 'giving it all', especially love.

★   ★   ★

I went missing in action in my marriage and the early days of parenthood, and I was cast further adrift in the Sandwich Years. I had lost myself. It happens. It happens to women all the time. Life takes up all our time. But my life now faced a new beginning. A certain peace had descended around me regarding my mum. My marriage was over and I faced a new future. As I started to draw my own map, little by little, I found bits of myself along the road (oh look, there's my brain. Oh wait, did we just drive past my figure? Wait, why am I wearing my mother's clothes?). So I started to build myself up again. My mum might have been stuck in time during the Sandwich Years, but I was a work very much progressing, as wrinkles and sun-saggy chest skin demonstrated. Weirdly, since my mum's stroke, she was no longer pained by arthritis and her skin was in a wonderful condition. A testament to the amazing carers that came in every day to wash her was that she never had a single bed sore in five years. She has no bags under her eyes and her cheeks filled out with Dad's good cooking and bed rest. In some horrible third dimension of sliding doors, my mum has started to look younger while I look older. Really, life, that's just an insult too far.

Part of climbing back was to get fit enough to make the ascent. I had first gone running as a teenager with my dad, who had given up a 60-a-day smoking habit and taken up a marathon-a-year habit. Once I had children I took it up again to help lose baby weight. At first I started running to get away from my life: screaming kids, chocolate cupboards, needs, needs, needs. Slowly, I began to see it as my time, and I enjoyed the space it gave me away from everything that rested on my shoulders. Then, on my forty-fourth birthday, after talking about it for years, I got an email from my wonderful friend Carol. My present was a registration for the Dublin marathon. She was going to help me go for my dream of running past our house (mile 16) on the biggest personal challenge of my life. I ran, and I trained and I raised money for the stroke unit that helped my mum. I had some of the hardest physical moments of my life, some of the most brutal mental moments of my life, and some of the most exhilarating moments of my life. And they were all mine.

I wasn't doing it for anyone else but myself. The training took a huge commitment of time, but something very important happened. Or rather didn't happen. I took out the time for *me* and the world did not cave in. That was a very important lesson to learn. I took time for me and no-one complained, went unfed or died. As Carol and I trained, our feet pounding the ground, our jaws got as much exercise as our legs as we performed marathon sessions of talking. We pushed each other, and friendship got us through it, along with a few cold baths. However, until I crossed the finish line on marathon day, I never really believed I could do it. It was such an impossible goal because I had always restricted myself to believing I could only ever run 10 km. But training for the marathon forced me to face my fear and raise my limits, and although I got a medal at the end, it was the internal prize that meant the most. The knowledge that I could get rid of my limits, and re-write the outlines, and push myself beyond all expectations. I became fitter than I had ever been in my life, and not just physically. It took as much mental strength as muscle strength and I started to realise I could raise my limits so much more.

They call it middle age, but I prefer to say I am right in the middle of my life. I am deliberately ignoring the official statistics that say I am actually beyond my middle. I hate being a statistic. I think middle is a good word. It means only half way. It's like I've sat the tests for the last forty-five years and now I get to graduate, armed and ready for life. Let me learn, let me live, let me love. Middle also means you are often surrounded by something, sandwiched between love, be that for parents, children, partners or friends. I am at a really exciting point in my life. It is the middle, and everything is changing. For many years I drifted — in a difficult marriage, in a pit of grief, in a fury of frenetic domestic chores — and I am now done with drifting. I want to live my life with purpose and intent.

As I write this, it is September, five years

exactly since my Sandwich Years began. We have been through so much as a family, but we are at peace now. We have loved and gone through the loss and know that whatever happens with Mum, we have done and will do our best for her. With my marriage over I embark on another new phase of life, limping slightly but building back those muscles. The heat from the summer sun is diminishing in strength. It's a little chillier, night comes a little earlier in the day. I apply sun cream in the morning, and light the fire in the evening. Autumn is tapping its feet in impatience and the air, promising to bluster the dying blossoms away, is also, as Nora Ephron wrote, scented by the 'bouquet of newly sharpened pencils'. Change is chomping at the bit as the girls and I prepare to swap summer for school, but the feeling of newness is as crisp as the white blouses I have bought in three different sizes. It's not just the season that is changing. My whole life is. As the school bells ring out on a new school year, they ring in a new phase. For ten years I have had a baby or small child at home. But I laid out a uniform for my last child and for the first time I labelled three schoolbags as they excitedly packed their pencil cases. All my babies are now schoolgirls. A whole new phase of life.

But the biggest change is in me. I am back to me but have gathered three glorious gifts on the way, and a lot of lessons. I am back to me, but a better me: less selfish and more self-focused; scarred but strengthened; battered but not beaten; stripped and stretched but more layered and filled out; poorer but richer; alone but alive; uncertain but aware; hurt but happier. I am more caring, and less tolerant. I want to act the fool more, and suffer fools less. I want deep, crunchy, liberating, intoxicating, exhilarating conversations with lots of interesting people, and quiet cuddles in bed with my girls. For many years, sandwiched in this storm of responsibility caring for my husband's needs, my parents' needs, my childrens' needs, house and home and work needs, I lost track of who I was. But I feel I am closing a door on all that confusion. I have realised that I have needs too. I'll take a rucksack filled with the goodness of that time, and leave the debris of destruction on the floor. As the yellow summer sun does a dazzling dance with the golden autumn glow before drifting away for another year, I am stepping through a door into a whole new phase of life. I like the look of the one I am opening. I am a daughter still, a mother always, a friend to amazing people, a businesswoman and a writer. But rising above all of those labels, I am me. It is all change. Parts of that change are painful, but necessary. Parts of that change are frightening but worth it. Parts of that change are exciting, and bursting with opportunity. Part of it is about letting go, and part of it is about grasping new things. It's a bittersweet mix but I'm ready . . . a whole new phase of life.

I think many women spend a good chunk of their lives exhausted and overwhelmed.

I've certainly spent the last 10 years exhausted as a parent. I've spent the last five years grief-stricken and overwhelmed, as a parent and a daughter, often feeling I was living my life at half-mast. But I want to raise my flag again and know that I can take the buffeting. I'm exhausted but energised. I am in the middle of my life but I feel I am just getting going.

When I was in my twenties I wrote myself a letter. I was sitting in the middle of a rainforest in Borneo and it felt so spectacular I wanted to make sure I never forgot that feeling. It was a moment that felt so right I wanted to bottle it up, so I took out an airmail sheet and began to write to myself. I wrote about the loudness of the silence. The vastness of the trees, so tall they formed a canopy overhead that blotted out the sky. The splashes of the raindrops dripping from leaves

I couldn't see. The cacophony of insects playing a vibrant melody that sang of life. I had an amazing life of adventure, and I told myself to never forget that moment. Of course, I immediately forgot that moment. A year passed with lots more amazing moments as I travelled and worked across Southeast Asia and New Zealand. So, when I eventually set my rucksack down in my Belfast bedroom, broke, jobless and adventureless, there it was. A blue tissue envelope sitting on my childhood homework desk. I recognised the writing but couldn't place it. Then I sat on my bed, opened it and read my own words to myself. I read my words and closed my eyes and felt myself back in that moment, in that rainforest. I could hear the noise and feel the pressure of humidity prickling my skin, see that every twine of leaf and stem had a purpose and a focus in that jumble of jungle. I remembered. What I will never forget though is the power of my own words, and how they affected me that day. I think it was the first time I realised I had power within me to power myself on.

As I sit now in the jumble of the jungle of my new life, I wonder what I would write to myself. What have I learned from the adventures and misadventures of my life? I think I would write, 'Stand up and put your face on . . . but know when to sit down and have a cup of tea, with a little bit of something nice.' I would remind myself that time is precious and to spend it on the things, and people, that matter. I would write that life is full of impermanence and that grief is a natural and inevitable part of it. Grief can't be figured out from a book. Instead, it has to be felt, lived, invited into your home. It will come and go, and become a part of you. It is not something to solve but absorb, and in the hangover of grief, you will have scars but also memories and you will experience real joy again. I would really remind myself to make room for that joy. My mum's loss made me a better parent. It woke me up to how temporary we all are. I want to make memories as well as the school lunches. I want to laugh more than I shout, and more than pretty much anything else, I want to love.

Life can indeed be a tricky old witch, but she is also a teacher and a friend. I would write that the thing about life is that it is a challenge. But that challenges are good as well as bad. The good enriches us, and the bad teaches us and allows us to know ourselves better. Life is sweet and bitter, fraught and fragile, full of joy. The most difficult times for many of us are actually the times we give ourselves. I would write in block capital letters:

LIFE IS HARD. BE KIND TO YOUR-SELF.

I would tell myself to trust the map that is formed from all the meandering roads and paths I have taken, and use it to forge new ground. That a map gives you a fixed point on the horizon — a place to work towards. So even when I am wading through the mud I need to keep moving forward. Even if the steps are slow and heavy having a fixed light helps me reach for a better time. I would remind myself that during the terrible days of Mum's stroke, some moments were so awful I would close my eyes and picture myself on a beach with the sun on my face, knowing some day I would feel that sun. And I did. I would remind myself that when my marriage ended someone told me I had the right to choose happiness, and that that carried me through those shock-filled days until I was able to fix my light on the horizon — one where we still had a family that our children could thrive in and be proud of. I would remind myself that when the tsunami of anger and grief hit, I was able to keep the light in my sights. I was able to live the anger and grief, standing in the mire and muck of hurt in the safety of knowing I had a better place to get to. Those words helped keep me on track. They were the words in the sky every day I pulled back the curtains, words that helped me decide how that day might be and that helped me put my face on. They helped me know that I would get through this eventually if I stayed true to myself. They helped me keep the children's needs uppermost, but also, to look after my own. I would remind myself that sometimes that guiding light came from over my shoulder, from the past and the love I have been given. Sometimes it shone on me from the future, a place to aim for. And sometimes that light came from within me. I would write that while it's important to have a vision of where I want to go, that vision is not about arriving at a place where everything is perfect and I finally have got it together. That is not a place to aim for. Like my fantasy version of George Clooney, that place is a made-up Hollywood dream.

I would write that terrible things can happen, and that LIFE IS HARD SOME-TIMES, but I can still be happy. That happiness is not my situation, but my attitude. That I have resilience and inner courage. I have a legacy of love, and a chain full of links that will always keep me strong. I would tell myself to be kind. Not just to the friends and family around me, but to myself. I would tell myself to make sure that while I cared for other people, it was really important to care for me. That is what I would write to myself again, if I wrote another letter. But then again, I think I just did.

★ ★ ★

I was about 21 miles into the marathon when I hit the wall. It happens suddenly, when you run out of steam, and the lure of a nice cup of tea and a little bit of something nice makes you want to stop. Immediately. Dad had come down to Dublin to cheer me on, and I had already passed him and my girls cheering and waving a humongous banner outside our house at the 16-mile mark. Leaving them behind to make the last push was hard. Maybe it was the jellybean overdose from over-generous spectators, or the mere fact I'd run 21 miles, but something gave. At first it looked like it was my knee, but it turned out to be my will. My knee screamed in pain but I kept going and it receded but my head was screaming louder. I wanted to stop. I couldn't go on another step. I pushed myself to 22 miles and this time hit the hill. I was literally on my last legs, my last breath, my last ounce of energy. Knowing I had only about three or four miles to go but I couldn't make it was one of the most soul-destroying experiences of my life. I think I went into some sort of current-traumatic stress state. Carol was whispering words of support beside me, every word getting one more foot down, but I was zoning out. I started to get nauseous and dizzy and as I neared the top of the hill, I was close to passing out. And then I began to hallucinate.

Running towards me was a small knitted jumper. That was all I could see. It looked uncannily like a ludicrous, fluffy, multi-coloured thing my mum had knitted years ago for my niece, Ellie. The long-haired wool was made from merged colours so when it was knitted out it made the wearer look like a fluffy ball of vomited rainbow. Once Ellie outgrew it, my girls took it for their fancy dress box. But here it was. Running towards me from a crowd of people as I began to lose consciousness. My thoughts were so con-fused, and for a moment I just thought about my mum. Had she somehow sent this jumper to me in my moment of need? Then, just slightly, my vision cleared and I saw the jumper wasn't running on its own. It had a body inside it. My vision focused a bit more. The body was my daughter's. It WAS my mum's ludicrous jumper, and despite the fact that it was a warm sunny day, for some serendipitous reason, my daughter had pulled it out of the box and put it on. My vision cleared entirely and there stood my family. They had left mile 16 as soon as I had passed and drove like lunatics to cheer me on again nearer the finish line. I fell into my dad's arms and cried, 'I can't go on!'

He straightened me up and smiled.

'Yes, you can,' he said gently, but with an authority I knew well. 'Go.' I didn't want to leave. I wanted to collapse into my family and never have to move my feet again. But I looked at my dad, and my girls and my mum's ludicrous vomited rainbow jumper and I did go. It was the hardest hour of my life, but like her Lipstick Rewards from the swimming pool all those years before, she had given me the strength to carry on, when I had none left of my own.

I once tortured myself wondering how I would cope without my mum. I don't ask that question now because I don't have to. I'll always have her. She is in me. Her hand will guide me even when all I have left is her handprint on my bracelet. The charm I had made of her handprint no longer represents my loss, but what she has given me. It is no longer about grief but about strength.

Because I also have her handprint on my heart.

★   ★   ★

I sometimes go running in my local park. Beyond the main section, and all the football pitches and walkways is a little forest. It has an earthen path and the trees rise up along each side and their branches flutter in the wind, forming a sort of guard of honour as I pant past. I love running through that wood with the sounds of the stream trickling alongside. And in that wood there is a tree. I call it 'My Tree'. Like spaghetti on a plate, it has roots spaying out all around it, clutching deeply into the ground. Its trunk is solid and marked with time and weather. Sprouting from it are solid branches and from them smaller branches and then thin branches and from all of them leaves that hang on tight and make it so big and detailed. That tree is always changing, and yet it is always the same. In autumn it astounds me with its glowing colours of sun and gold. In winter it stands bare but coolly defiant against the chilling winds. In spring it sprouts with green and promise and in summer it glistens as the sun glitters through the gaps in its leaves. Its beauty always makes me stop.

Stop running, stop listening to podcasts, stop thinking. I just stop and gaze at it, and it always, always makes me feel better. It gives me my moment and for some reason always makes me feel grateful. Because it gives me something else. It reminds me of me. I am the trunk, but I am just the middle piece. I have deep-rooted beginnings and branches that sway into my future. All separate parts but all connected. I am mother, I am daughter, but sandwiched between the two, I am me, weathered and craggy but damn it, glorious and strong, always changing, always growing. I am finally starting to blossom. In reaching the middle of my life, I am becoming the woman I always wanted to be, and the woman I was always meant to be. The last ten years, in particular my Sandwich Years, in all their ups and downs, have been my evolution from a place unknown to a place where I know exactly who I want to be. Me. I am not afraid or ashamed of my strength anymore. I have found my place where I know and am proud that that strength is kindness, strength is love, strength is power, strength is asking for help, strength is caring for others, strength is caring for yourself, strength is ambition, strength is determination, strength is belief, strength is forgiveness, and strength is gentleness. I am strong because of the love I was given and the love that I am able to give. I can climb mountains, I can run marathons, I can write books, I can make change, I can ask for help, I can raise children, I can survive, I can thrive and I can make a mean macaroon. And I can do all of those things because of my mum, my family and the wonder of women on the chain I am part of.

For the last five years I have struggled and coped, survived and at times, eventually, even thrived, balancing the needs of lives flourishing and lives diminishing. Sandwiched between the loves of my life, I have been the filling. A squashed meat stuck between the breads of caring for young children and elderly, ailing parents. Much of the time I have felt like a limp petrol station pre-wrap. It has all the right elements but somehow it lacks flavour. But sometimes, eventually, I have felt a little gourmet. Creative, filling, full of flavour and bite. And often it was the very people who needed me that also nourished me.

There have been times I have needed my mum so badly I thought my very bones had broken. She can't say my name, but at times she can see my pain, and will lift the only part of her body she can move apart from her head, and put her hand against my cheek, and her eyes tell me it will be OK. And it *will* be OK. It *is* OK. I have survived the Sandwich

Years, perhaps only just. I have been dragged through the mill of life but I am coming out the other side. My bones have reset. They are wonkier perhaps, and are grooved with the mark of their wear. But strangely, they are stronger than they were. I wrote about my life as I stumbled and tumbled through the maze of bringing up young children, caring for sick parents and trying to come out the other side with a gin and a grin and a modicum of sanity. And although the people and places are personal to me, the predicament and pain are general to so many.

★   ★   ★

I'm a multi-platinum Oscar-holding statistic: I'm part of the Sandwich Generation; I'm an 'older mother' with a trail of miscarriages behind me; I'm separated. But I am also unique because of the love and family and friends I have built around me. My mum was mine. My family is mine. My girls are mine. My friends are mine. And as well as these relationships, my passions, talents, ambitions and opportunities are mine. No statistic will stop me.

When you pull the curtains back and search the sky, you never know what the day will bring, good, bad, mundane or miraculous. I don't try and read it anymore, I just try to be ready for anything and everything, because I know life will throw anything and everything at me. I have to greet the gods of doom and drama head on, face the fiascos, fight the fight, keep moving forward, learning and loving. Enjoy the good. Be aware, be present, see what I have, not what I've lost. Turn my face to the sun and feel the warmth. Sometimes I don't like the now I am in, but I have to live it anyway, knowing that there were plenty of good times behind me, and plenty more in front of me. Losing my mum made me want to live life to the full, take the bad with the good, so that my life is not defined by the bad but by the good. I want to look, listen, feel, see, be. But most of all, I want to choose happiness.

I am not religious but I do believe in the holy trinity that my mum lived by — the holy trinity of love, family and friends. My mum spent her time on people, and we are all happy and privileged to now spend time on her. I don't have a perfect mum, but that doesn't matter. I have a mum who loves me and has given me her time. I'm not a perfect mum, and I'm not sure I want to be. I want to be flawed just enough that they know it's OK to get it wrong, that giving it your all is better than having it all, that life is a struggle and sometimes you win and sometimes you flounder. But that you can get up and put your face on and keep going. One story does not define us. Where we have tragedy, we also have moments of laughter and love. Where we have loss, we also have moments of gain and realisation. No-one has one story. We are all made up of many, many stories. We can always redraw the map, reappoint the dotted lines. At the risk of sounding Buddhist, nothing is permanent. It's not so much about loss or about gain. It's about living the best way we can with whatever comes our way. Everything in life is an evolution, a revolution, a revelation, a renovation. Letting go, and climbing back and holding on, and moving on, are all necessary steps.

More than five years on, I still miss my mum deeply, and her role as the person who cared for me most. The person who cleaned my cooker top, who made me sit down and have a cup of tea with a little bit of something nice alongside, to hug me and hold my hand. But life has taught me to care for myself now instead. The Sandwich Years have been about learning to stand on my own two feet. But I was only able to do that by feeling the army of footprints behind me, by seeing the footprints in the sand that walk beside me, by watching the little footprints run off ahead of me, and feeling a hand always holding mine. My Sandwich Years continue to be tough, but they are also a privilege: to be sandwiched between my mum who taught me to love, and my girls who teach me to live. A love sandwich in which I am the filling of fortune.

I have a new plan. To live life the best way I can, even when it's really hard. I'm not striving for perfection, but I am striving for happiness. My plan involves living, loving and sitting down to drink cups of Earl Grey tea with a little bit of something nice on the side. My plan involves caring for those I care about, and being kind to myself. Because in the end, the only thing that matters, the only thing that is left behind, is love.

Acknowledgements

A good life is not lived alone, as a book is not written alone. So my thanks and love to:

all the women who went before me, who laid down my path;
and all the women who stand beside me, who shine a light on my path:

The amazing women who keep me sane and safe:

my wing-woman, Amanda, for always being my life-saver, and life-enricher;

my Wednesday crew mate Liza, for being the apple of my life (and cleaning my cooker top);

Julia, for being my sister, in every way;

Carol, for always pushing me, and then catching me too;

Jules, for knowing and loving me long and true;

my book club women, for the laughs, the wine and the occasional book talk.

The amazing women who safeguard the breads of my sandwich:

Meabh, for coming into our lives, and staying;

Pat and Hilary, for loving my mum, and now loving me and my girls too — thanks for making me an honorary member of The Girls;

Evelyn, for giving my mum an ear when she needed it, and for giving me one now too.

The amazing women who help me write:

Ciara Doorley for spotting my potential and helping me to see it, and all the team at Hachette Books Ireland for your guidance;

Sallyanne Sweeney at Mulcahy Associates for all your support and encouragement;

fellow writers and Emergency Support

Squad — Hazel Gaynor, Natasha Fennell, Sharon Thompson and Sue Leonard for their advice and shouts of 'Keep going!';

Vanessa O'Loughlin for believing in me, giving me direction and getting me there.

All the amazing carers who have looked after my mum so well — you are such heroes.
My 'carer' Kathleen, for your kind eyes and smile (and no South American pipe music).

The amazing men, who help me through life:
my brother for being the best man I know (and Charlotte for being the best sister-in-law);
and my dad, for keeping our family together and giving me a love of words.

But most of all, to the most amazing women in my life.
My flower girls:
Daisy, already I can see the smart, funny, ambitious woman you will be;
Poppy, already I can see the kind, imaginative, determined woman you will be;
Ruby Rose, already I can see the dynamic, loving and curious woman you will be.

And to my mum, for everything.

I am proud to have come from such a woman, and to raise such women. It is truly a sandwich of privilege.

Endnotes

1   Central Statistics Office, Health and Research Board and Information Division 2010

2   Office for National Statistics

3   Perinatal Statistics Report, ESRI, 2012

4   The Carers Association, according to the 2011 census

5   WHO: The Mayo Clinic

6   www.mumsnet.com

7   *Personality and Social Psychology Review*, Report by Sanctuary Spa, August 2015

Useful Websites

www.carersireland.com
www.caringforcarers.ie
www.carersassociation.ie
www.ageaction.ie
www.carersuk.org
www.nationalcareassociation.org.uk
www.carers.org

For support and information from the HSE
— http:// www.hse.ie/eng/services/list/4/ olderpeople/
For support and information from the NHS
— http: / / www.nhs.uk/Conditions/social-care-
and-support-guide / Pages / carers-assessment.aspx

We do hope that you have enjoyed reading this large print book.

Did you know that all of our titles are available for purchase?

We publish a wide range of high quality large print books including:
Romances, Mysteries, Classics
General Fiction
Non Fiction and Westerns

Special interest titles available in large print are:
The Little Oxford Dictionary
Music Book
Song Book
Hymn Book
Service Book

Also available from us courtesy of Oxford University Press:
Young Readers' Dictionary
(large print edition)
Young Readers' Thesaurus
(large print edition)

For further information or a free brochure, please contact us at:
Ulverscroft Large Print Books Ltd.,
The Green, Bradgate Road, Anstey,
Leicester, LE7 7FU, England.
Tel: (00 44) 0116 236 4325
Fax: (00 44) 0116 234 0205

Other titles published by Ulverscroft:

LEAP IN

Alexandra Heminsley

Alexandra Heminsley thought she could swim. She really did. It may have been because she could run, or because she only ever did ten minutes of breaststroke at a time. But, as she learned one day while flailing about in the sea, she really couldn't . . . Believing that the life lived most fully is the one with the most experience packed in, she decides to conquer her fear of the ocean tides. From the ignominy of getting into a wetsuit to the triumph of swimming from Kefalonia to Ithaca, Alex learns that the water is never as frightening once you're in . . .